KU-630-893

5

6/09

The French Book

Johns Hopkins Symposia in Comparative History

The Johns Hopkins Symposia in Comparative History are occasional volumes sponsored by the Department of History at the Johns Hopkins University and the Johns Hopkins University Press comprising original essays by leading scholars in the United States and other countries. Each volume considers, from a comparative perspective, an important topic of current historical interest. The present volume is the twenty-second. Its preparation has been assisted by the James S. Schouler Lecture Fund.

The French Book

RELIGION, ABSOLUTISM, AND READERSHIP, 1585–1715

Henri-Jean Martin

TRANSLATED BY
PAUL SAENGER AND
NADINE SAENGER

THE JOHNS HOPKINS UNIVERSITY PRESS
BALTIMORE AND LONDON

© 1996 The Johns Hopkins University Press
All rights reserved. Published 1996
Printed in the United States of America on acid-free paper
05 04 03 02 01 00 99 98 97 96   5 4 3 2 1

The Johns Hopkins University Press
2715 North Charles Street
Baltimore, Maryland 21218-4319
The Johns Hopkins Press Ltd., London

Library of Congress Cataloging-in-Publication Data will be found
at the end of this book.

A catalog record for this book is available from the British Library.

ISBN 0-8018-5179-3

Warm thanks are due to the Photographic Service of the Bibliothèque
Nationale for figures 1–5, 8, 12, 15, 17, 18, 20, 22–24, 26–29, and 33–38.

Contents

Illustrations

Figures

vii

Illustrations

Maps

Graphs

Foreword

Only rarely in the discipline of history is it possible to discern exactly when a whole new approach, or new subject, becomes a field of inquiry. That is precisely what happened, however, when Lucien Febvre and Henri-Jean Martin copublished *L'Apparition du Livre,* in the prestigious Evolution de l'Humanité series at Editions Albin Michel. The history of the book as a distinct subject and requiring its own approaches and methods dates from the publication of that book—this single inspiring work—in a Western culture heretofore having only bibliographical studies and antiquarian research on books.

In 1969 Martin extended and made bolder still the parameters of the new field by publishing *Livre, Pouvoir et Société à Paris au XVIIe siècle* (Geneva: Droz, 1969). There in 1,091 pages plus graphs lay the thematic analyses, the market trends, and the institutionalization of royal controls over publishing in one single grandiose work, and for a century of Parisian history.

Henri-Jean Martin and I met on the monumental steps of the Fine Arts Museum in Marseille in June 1991. He had heard of me from conversations with Professor Paul Saenger, a former student of mine from Columbia College days, and now a senior historian of the book at the Newberry Library. I was very familiar with Martin's work and admired it enormously. After a brief but quite eloquent compliment about his thesis, I asked, "Would you write up your thesis today in the same way as you did in the 1960s?" Martin replied instantly, "No, I would do it entirely differently." This answer became the premise for the invitation to give the Schouler Lectures at the Johns Hopkins University in the autumn of 1993. In addition to the sheer joy of learning from hearing and discussing the lectures that have become this book, Henri-Jean Martin and his wife, Odile, became friends and Baltimoreans. Their zest for urban life was particularly evident in their nearly endless walks all over the city.

The history of the book as a field of scholarship now has its specialists in universities, research centers, and libraries all over the world. It is a pleasure to recognize how the *world* of books is now taking on ever more precise historical contours as the geographic world becomes smaller as a result of the revolution in telecommunications.

A word of thanks is also in order for the work of Professor Paul Saenger and his wife, Nadine, who proceeded with care and erudition at every step in the translation and editing of these lectures.

Orest Ranum
Baltimore

The French Book

CHAPTER I

The Catholic Reformation and the Book (1585–1650)

Permit me, by way of introduction, to take you into a printing shop. Let us look, for example, at a famous engraving by the Flemish engraver Van der Straet depicting a printing shop from the end of the sixteenth century (fig. 1). On the right, in front of the master printer, who surveys the work, a journeyman maneuvers the press bar to produce the impression. Behind the first press, another journeyman uses balls of leather to ink the form of a second press. Above him, the sheets of paper, moistened prior to printing, are drying. In the foreground at the center of the engraving, an apprentice standing in front of a table stacks the sheets of paper as they dry. On the left, type-setters, seated before the type case in front of small windows, compose their text from a manu-script placed before them attached to a *visorium*. At the same time, another compiler works be-hind a pillar, and near him the corrector or the author stands proofreading the copy.

IMPRESSIO LIBRORVM.

Potest vt vna vox capi aure plurima: *Linunt ita vna scripta mille paginas.*

Fig. 1. A printing shop

This engraving gives us a fairly good idea of the crowded conditions in which printers carried out their tasks. The yields that they were supposed to attain appear frighteningly high. In fact, corporate rules demanded that 2,500 to 3,000 leaves recto or verso be printed during workdays that lasted as long as 14 hours.[1] In addition, even the best printing shops had at their disposal only a limited quantity of type. It was therefore necessary to print each form as soon as it was composed so that the type could be cleaned for immediate reuse. The result was that the proofreading often took place while the printing was in progress, and noticeable divergences between copies occurred. The eminent American and English specialists of the science known as analytical bibliography, who are well aware of this phenomenon, take these divergences into account when an early printed text is critically edited.[2]

Moreover, the number of copies of each edition was conditioned by the same economic and technical imperatives common to all mass production. The need to reduce unit costs obviously required a printing run large enough to be able to spread the fixed expenses—in particular, those for the composition of the text and the engraving of the illustrations—over a large number of copies. Nevertheless, it was important not to print too many copies, thereby tying up for too long a time the capital needed for the purchase of paper, which represented an important expenditure. These considerations explain why the number of copies in a pressrun of the same type of book remained relatively fixed in a given time and place. To be more concrete, let us say that in the fifteenth century, the production of a single book amounted to 500 copies and in the sixteenth century to 1,000 copies. For the period that interests us, Christopher Plantin published most of his editions in numbers ranging from 1,000 to 1,500 copies, and, particularly in the seventeenth century, the original editions of French literary texts normally varied between 1,200 and 1,800 copies. Of course, it must be understood that if a work were successful, it would be reprinted immediately. In certain cases, however, editions could either attain 2,500 or 3,000 copies or be restricted to a run of 750 or 800.[3]

If one discounts a few exceptional cases such as that of the printing shop of the Plantin-Moretus at Antwerp, the shops of this period rarely contained more than six presses. These were used not only to print books but also to perform printing for the municipalities—that is, to print posters and administrative and legislative documents, as well as reports addressed to tribunals. Such commissions provided a steady source of income to certain shops, notably those located in cities that as printing centers were of medium or lesser importance.

In the course of this period certain cities established themselves as important publishing centers. Map 1 reflects all the sixteenth-century works preserved at the British Library. Certainly, recourse to this institutional collection as a source is open to question because it leads to an overemphasis of the role of scholarly and literary publications that are better repre-

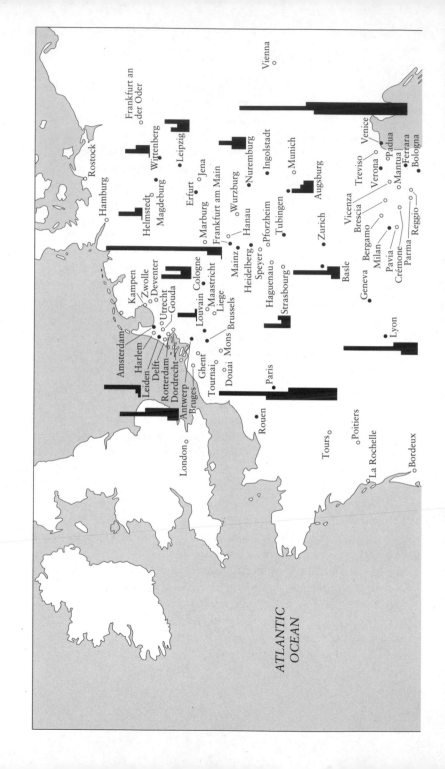

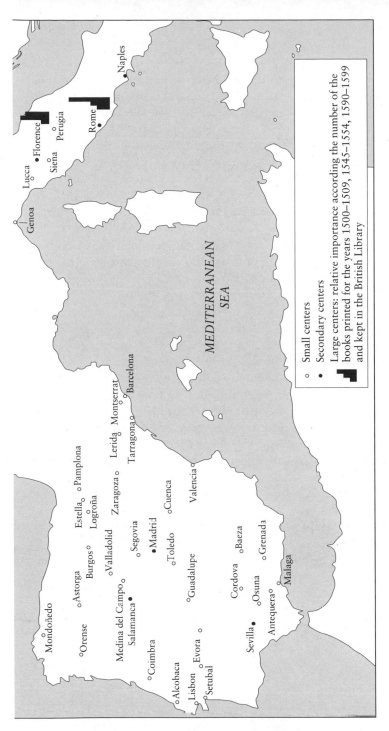

Map 1. Large publishing centers in Europe in the sixteenth century

Small centers ○
Secondary centers ●
Large centers: relative importance according the number of the books printed for the years 1500–1509, 1545–1554, 1590–1599 and kept in the British Library

MEDITERRANEAN
SEA

Naples
Rome
Perugia
Siena
Florence
Lucca
Genoa

Barcelona
Montserrat
Tarragona
Lerida
Pamplona
Estella
Logroña
Zaragoza
Valencia
Cuenca
Segovia
Madrid
Toledo
Baeza
Grenada
Cordova
Malaga
Osuna
Antequera
Sevilla
Guadalupe
Medina del Campo
Salamanca
Valladolid
Burgos
Astorga
Orense
Mondoñedo
Coimbra
Alcobaca
Lisbon
Evora
Setubal

sented than utilitarian books. Nevertheless, a certain number of conclusions can be drawn. On the one hand, the importance of Venice is clear. It was without doubt the principal European publishing center throughout the sixteenth century. On the other hand, the relative insignificance of the rest of Italy is also evident. Spain, then in her apogee, appears to have been relatively unimportant, while two other centers, Lyon and Paris, dominated the French market, establishing themselves globally as the second and third largest European centers. In the Germanic countries, the growth of Frankfurt was evident at the end of the century. Note, finally, the development of centers in the Low Countries, of which the most notable was Antwerp (the city of Plantin) in midcentury and Leiden at the end of the century.

In the upper left corner of this map, the insert based on archival documents indicates the cities with which Lyon had commercial relations. This reminds us that the commerce of books, especially of Latin books, was for the most part international. Such commerce evidently posed very complex financial problems. As a general rule, bookseller-publishers bartered among themselves. Still, they had to meet regularly to settle their accounts, to pay their debts by a system of bills of exchange, and to agree upon future trades. Therefore these men voyaged frequently and saw each other regularly at book fairs. The Lyon fair seems to have played a considerable role in this regard.[4] However, in the last third of the sixteenth century, renewed peace favored the growing importance of the Frankfurt fair. There, books as well as horses, arms, and wine were sold. The catalogs of books placed on sale each year at Frankfurt were published regularly beginning in 1564. They give us an idea of the nature of the trade. Two-thirds of the books offered were in Latin. The bookstands of dealers from Catholic countries were next to those of Protestant countries. At the same time, non-German booksellers frequented these fairs in great numbers, coming not only from Paris and Lyon but also from Venice and in even greater numbers from the Low Countries, especially from Antwerp but increasingly also from the important cities of Leiden and Amsterdam (map 2).

With the aid of a few images, let us try to imagine what the life of the booksellers, binders, and printers that form the subject of this book may have been like. The book trades of the great French centers of Paris and Lyon were located in certain well-defined quarters of the city. At Lyon, they were located along the rue Mercière, the large mercantile street joining the bridge over the Saône to that of the Rhône and occupying a strategic commercial position. At Paris, the men of the book trades were traditionally grouped around the university. Important publishers and booksellers, like the sellers of engravings, had their shops along the rue Saint-Jacques, the great commercial street that formed an arterial route linking the valleys of the Loire and the Saône to Flanders. Booksellers were also situated along the rue de la Harpe, another relatively important commercial artery. In addition, many booksellers maintained their stalls at the Palais, the administrative and royal judicial center with its numerous courts—the Parlement, chambre des comptes, cour des aides, etc. It was there that specialized booksellers displayed the latest literary arrivals, and a famous illustration by Abraham Bosse, undoubtedly representing the stall of Augustin Courbé, gives us a fairly precise notion of the minuscule shops in which this commerce was carried out (fig. 2). Less well-known booksellers, binders, and printers were crammed together in the small streets of the Montagne-Sainte-Geneviève. There at the back of courtyards, an observer could catch a glimpse of a few of the two hundred presses that in about 1640 functioned in some seventy workshops.[5] In general, the atmosphere in this quarter seems to have been similar to that of the suqs of today's Moslem cities, as we can well imagine when we look at Paris's little-changed rue d'Écosse. There a statue of the Virgin (which unfortunately disappeared early in this century) towered over the *Puits Certain* where apprentices tradition-

7

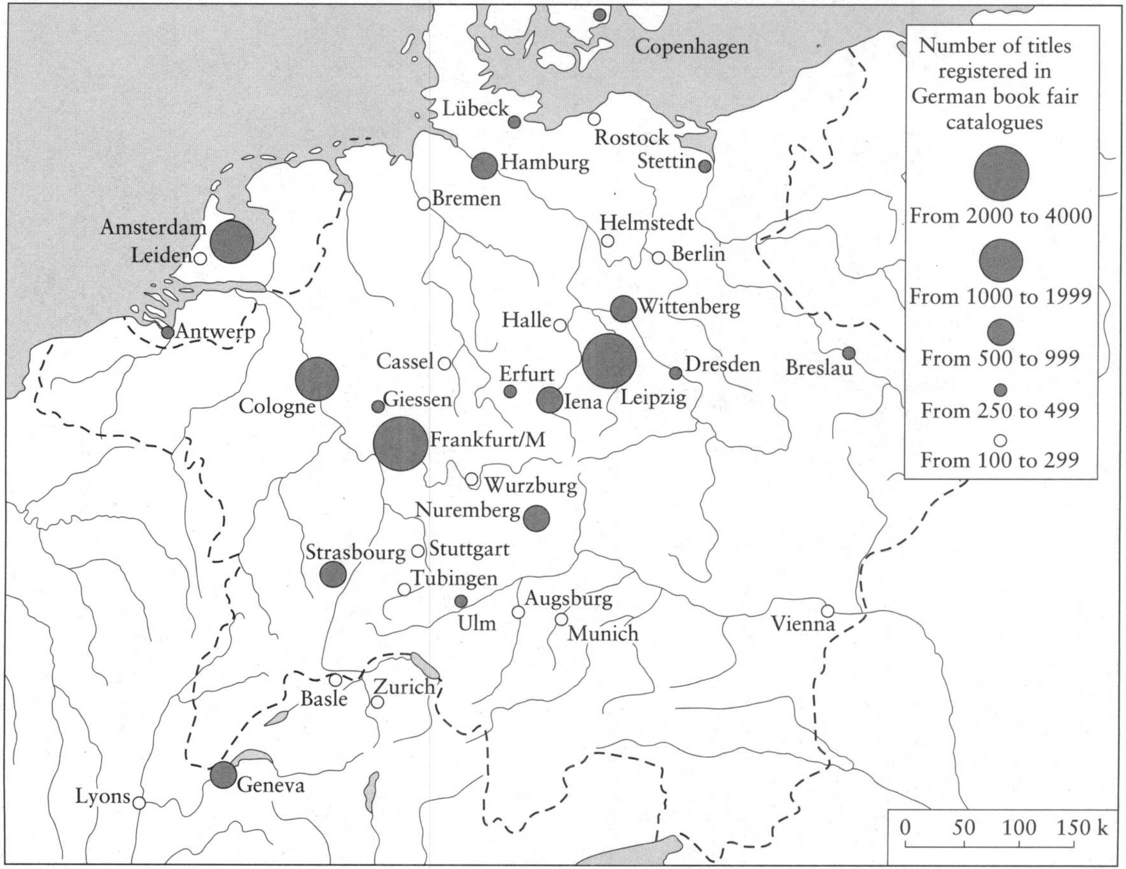
Number of titles registered in German book fair catalogues
From 2000 to 4000
From 1000 to 1999
From 500 to 999
From 250 to 499
From 100 to 299
0
50
100
150 k
Copenhagen
Lübeck
Rostock
Hamburg
Stettin
Bremen
Helmstedt
Berlin
Amsterdam
Leiden
Wittenberg
Halle
Antwerp
Cassel
Erfurt
Leipzig
Dresden
Breslau
Cologne
Giessen
Iena
Frankfurt/M
Wurzburg
Nuremberg
Strasbourg
Stuttgart
Tubingen
Augsburg
Ulm
Munich
Vienna
Basle
Zurich
Geneva
Lyons

Map 2. European booksellers in the Frankfurt and Leipzig fairs, 1601–25

Fig. 2. A bookseller's shop in the Palais

ally came to draw the water needed for washing their type. If the closeness of this existence sometimes encouraged gossiping and disputes, it also more often fostered a solidarity that at times greatly facilitated the printing and publication of pamphlets.

Finally, a great problem for the publishers was to ensure that the merchandise was delivered to their clients in good condition. To this end, booksellers proceeded in the same fashion as other merchants, as can be seen in other Flemish engravings. They shipped their products in barrels when they were bound volumes (fig. 3a), or in packages when the volumes were sent "in sheets" (fig. 3b), that is, unbound, as was usually the case. The sender was careful to place a symbol on the package denoting the addressee. The packages were then consigned to riverboats or carriages. They often arrived damaged, frequently wet, or were lost in the course of an eventful voyage, as

Fig. 3. The transport of books: *a,* the barrel of bound books; *b,* the package for books "in sheets"

De Ballenbinder.
Lüste so die Welt hie gibt, mache uns bey Gott beliebt

Das Werck der Ball aus Staub und Erde
das sich leicht blehet in dem Glück,
muß durch das Leid gerattelt werden,
damit es sich geschmeidig schick'
auff GOttes Wagen der nichts träget,
als was den Stolz hat abgeleget.

the surviving correspondence of merchants documents. These documents record sufficient details to show how risky the commerce of books was, as indeed was all long-distance commerce at this time.

A MOST REMARKABLE FACT of this period is assuredly the flooding of the market with an enormous quantity of religious tracts inspired by what is commonly referred to as the Counter-Reformation. At this point, we must briefly summarize the attitude of the Catholic Church vis-à-vis the printing press. Initially, the voice of the Church was heard in the concert of praise that welcomed the birth of printing. However, the Church soon became disenchanted. As early as 1479, a powerful consortium brought out the first Bible in Low German. Cologne theologians immediately alerted the papacy. Rome at once imposed on the printers of that great German city the requirement of obtaining prepublication permission. This system was gradually extended, and on the fourth of May 1515 the pope decided to apply it to all of Christendom.[6]

Thus, prepublication censorship was instituted even before Luther's appearance on the scene. Beginning in the year 1517, when the great heretic leader nailed his propositions condemning indulgences to the door of the Augustinian church in Wittenberg, the threat became real. Historians of the German book insist that the outpouring of pamphlets—printed in quarto format, of shorter length than ordinary theology books, and often accompanied by caricatures—corresponded to a true psychological revolution, the molding of public opinion in a Germany that had already become largely literate. It was the printing press that for the first time guaranteed the success of this new mission.

I shall skip over the numerous widespread measures taken subsequently to try to stem the multiplication of works, especially pamphlets, judged to be pernicious by the Catholic Church. But we must take note of some of the decisions taken at the beginning of the Council of Trent (which ended in 1564), decisions that had enormous consequences for printing. In order to cut short all controversy, the fathers assembled at the council decided to proclaim the Vulgate, that is, the Latin text of the Bible as established by Jerome, to be the authentic version of Holy Scripture. Other versions could be consulted only to explicate its meaning. It was likewise decided to carefully revise the Roman liturgy to make local liturgies, so often denounced by Protestants as laden with superstition, consistent with a new standard.

At the same time, Rome struggled to take the lead in applying the policy of repression that had been developing almost everywhere. The result was the publication, in 1564, of an Index of prohibited books kept carefully up to date by a special commission. It contained a list of the works of the leading heretics and heretical works of others who were not Protestants, for example, those of Erasmus. The Index condemned these works either forever or *donec corrigatur* (until they shall be corrected). This left open the possibility of producing purged editions or of letting complete editions circulate in which the condemned passages were obliterated by ink. Moreover, a bull of 24 March 1564 published ten rules for the Index. In particular, this bull forbade the faithful to read translations of Scripture without the permission of the prelate or the inquisitor of the region who could act only after having consulted the confessor or priest of the interested party. The reading of controversial books and even of the ancient classics was regulated. Finally, the tenth rule reiterated the obligation to obtain authorization prior to all publication and invited the bishop of the region or his rightful representative to visit printers' shops and bookstores on a regular basis.[7]

Such measures might of course shock the sensibilities of modern men, especially Protestants. I shall limit myself here to underscoring the fact that these events resulted from an important principle of the Catholic Church, namely, that only a priest was competent to interpret and explain divine intentions and religious mysteries on the basis of tradition, the heritage transmitted from generation to generation by the apostles and their successors the bishops. This is a theory that has profoundly marked the mentality of the French, who, as the country has become more secular, have curiously transferred this form of priestly authority to writers and intellectuals who still today are unconsciously viewed as possessors of moral and intellectual power.

Regardless of the consequences, the pope, on the basis of these rules, intended to endow himself with a formidable power. Clearly even the most Catholic sovereigns could not allow the Church to exercise censorship in their countries, and therefore they always tried to control their own printers and to determine what should be prohibited within their own domains. Therefore the pontifical initiatives led secular scholars to organize their own system of censorship, a subject to which we shall return in a future chapter. Henceforth, however, Rome became the dispenser of texts of extraordinary import, namely its own revised version of the Vulgate, and, even more significantly, standardized service books, the works required for celebrating the divine offices, such as missals, breviaries, and antiphonaries. These were repeatedly revised and after each revision reintroduced into all the churches of Catholic Christendom.[8] Desirous of controlling every publication in order to prevent textual corruptions, the popes envisaged entrusting publications to printers of their own choosing. However, here as well, it was necessary to yield to the temporal authorities, a topic to which we shall also return.

Such measures would hardly have been of consequence if they had not been accompanied by a renewal of faith in Catholic countries—which explains why I prefer to label this movement the Catholic Reformation. The attempt to revise doctrine, which had begun much earlier, blossomed during this period under the aegis of the Jesuits who, by means of their universities and colleges, undertook responsibility for educating the elite. To some degree everywhere, but especially in France, the old religious orders reformed themselves, new orders appeared, and convents were constructed thanks to donations of money and abundant bequests.

An essential fact is that all these reforms and creations of ecclesiastical institutions were accompanied by the construction of libraries conceived of as weapons for the reconquest of souls. In these libraries, the ponderous volumes of renovated theology were crammed together. Until about 1630, however, most of these books were the work of foreign scholars in France. These included Italians such as the illustrious Cardinal Bellarmino and Cardinal Baronius, the author of the *Annales,* who aimed to show that the Church followed the same path, century after century, contrary to the claims of the Protestants. There were also Flemings, like Cornelius a Lapide (in the vernacular Cornelius Van der Steen), author of a weighty commentary on Scripture consisting of some twenty folio volumes. Spaniards such as the renovators of Thomist philosophy Suarez and Vasquez, theologians such as Toledo, Maldonado, Ribera, Azor, and Sa, theoreticians of ultramontane political theology, and defenders of tyrannicide such as Mariana or Santarelli were also prominent.

Characteristically, these highly saleable works were distributed on the basis of a well-conceived strategy worked out between the important centers of Catholic publishing: Cologne and Mainz for Germany, Venice for Italy, Antwerp for Flanders, and Paris and Lyon for France. Paris became the metropolis for the publication of patristic editions and biblical commentaries that were not susceptible to criticism by the Gallicans, the partisans of the independence of the church of France, who were particularly numerous in the Parlement and at the Sorbonne. In contrast Spanish theologians, notably the casuist-authors of treatises that determined the gravity of sins and their ensuing punishments (works that were often thought to be too lax by their adversaries, such as Pascal in his *Lettres provinciales*), preferred to have their texts printed in Lyon, a city with a strategic position in Europe that was well removed from royal authority.

It is not without interest to note that for obvious reasons works of political theology were only edited in Spain.[9]

Undoubtedly, the publishers and booksellers to whom these books were entrusted were carefully chosen, and they acted as trusted confidants. Such was the role, in particular, of Christopher Plantin at Antwerp. An emigrant from France, he succeeded in creating an important printing establishment in this port city that had become the hub of the Occident. To raise the capital for this enterprise he first turned to members of the heterodox sects. However, when Flanders was definitively reconquered by Spain, he went into the service of the Counter-Reformation for which he printed, most notably, his famous polyglot Bible, of which the text had been reviewed by Arias Montanus, the chaplain of Philip II. Subsequently, Plantin and the Moretus family, his successors, became both the editors of the stoic philosopher Justus Lipsius and the printers of innumerable theological texts, especially the liturgical books destined for all the territories dominated by Spain. This immense market explains why Plantin's shop sometimes had as many as twenty presses operating at one time.[10]

It is understandable that Plantin and his foreign imitators, such as the Parisian Sébastien Cramoisy (to whom we shall return) and the Lyonnais Horace Cardon, were engaged in an extremely fruitful commerce in more than one country that tended to exclude publishers and booksellers from Protestant countries. Protestants in the Low Countries and Germany tried to protect themselves by specializing in scholarly editions of the ancient classics. Above all else, they were forced to be innovative. Thus, at a time when the conquest of distant lands was the order of the day, the publishers and booksellers of Amsterdam specialized in the publication of large atlases by perfecting the techniques of copperplate engraving. Others in London or around Frankfurt published numerous collections of travel stories, which were often illustrated. In particular, the Elzevirs at Leiden and Amsterdam took advantage of the improvements in printing occurring in their country to bring out, in small format, finely printed elegant collections of the standard classical texts, the works of the great humanists, and descriptions of European countries (the series of the Republics). These were soon followed by the texts of the most famous French writers, such as Charron and Corneille, as well as books placed on the Index or for other cause forbidden in the Catholic countries.[11]

Just as the Counter-Reformation formulated a new theology, its renewal of religiosity stimulated the appearance of a new spiritual literature. It developed first in Italy and especially in Spain. For a long time, however, the fear of unorthodox doctrinal deviations such as Illuminism led the Spanish prelates to avoid diffusing new spiritual works. The great inquisitor Fernando de Valdes censured, for example, the works of the Dominican Luis de Grenada. The *Spiritual Exercises* of Ignatius of Loyola only barely escaped the Spanish Index, and for this reason Theresa of Avila's works were circulated for a long time in manuscript. Under these conditions, the French spiritual renewal, encouraged at the time by the Ligue's Guise leaders and especially by the Cardinal of Lorraine, was at first nourished by the traditional reprintings of the classics of Rhéno-Flemish spirituality, notably the works of Nider and Suso, and, most important, the *De imitatione Christi,* which soon became the best seller par excellence of seventeenth-century France.

This situation explains why early French Carmelites, grouped around Madame Acarie in Paris, engaged in essentially abstract spiritual exercises and expressed surprise when companions of Theresa of Avila, who in 1601 were brought from Spain by the young abbot of Bérulle (the future cardinal and founder of the *Oratoire*), taught the use of concrete images in their pursuit of God. From then on, French piety was nourished by Spanish models. The *Life of Saint Theresa* became the Bible of the devout, while the *Spiritual Catechism* of Luis de Grenada began its exceptional popularity, which eventually spread across Europe. At the same time, the spiritual works of the Spanish Jesuits inundated France. Gradually, however, during this period, which French historians have labeled the "Age of the Saints," French spiritual authors also appeared. Among them I shall only mention here François de Sales, who, in the *Introduction à la vie dévote*, instructed men and women who could not retreat from this world how to assure salvation while remaining fully engaged in secular affairs.[12]

Thus, the renewal of Catholic piety developed along essentially emotional lines on the basis of a hierarchically ordered didactic literature composed of saints' lives, catechisms, meditations, and spiritual exercises of all types. In contrast, the reading of the Bible remained inaccessible to the faithful who were ignorant of Latin, a state of affairs that would continue until the Jansenists succeeded in bringing this exclusion to an end after prolonged battles fought during the second half of the seventeenth century.

It is not difficult to imagine that in such a climate, theologians and spiritual authors were forced to be explicit and to reinforce their texts with the allegorical images that had been employed since antiquity and that had been subsequently disseminated by means of patristic texts, encyclopedias, and allegorical compilations. Authors, such as Valeriano and Ripa and their successors, devoted themselves to compiling and purging the traditional corpus of its pagan elements. This effort culminated in the publication of illustrated repertories that offered a rigorous codification for the use of allegory. Cardinal Paleotti exalted the excellence of symbolism in his *De imaginibus sacris et profanis* in which he reminded the reader of Augustine's dictum that all creations evoke something of their creator, and citing Albertus Magnus and Thomas Aquinas, he emphasized that material creatures symbolize the wisdom and goodness of God.[13] Thus, since it was believed that man could use the visible to arrive at knowledge of the invisible, it is not surprising both that Rubens designed for the Moretus, the successors of Plantin, frontispieces often full of very complex allegories and that the technique of emblems was widely applied to the illustration of spiritual books. I shall return to this point in my last chapter. As a result, during this period, theological and spiritual literature provided printers and booksellers with most of their work. It is not surprising, therefore, that they proved to be very obedient to the wishes of the Church, which guaranteed them both texts to publish and a clientele to purchase them. It is also not surprising that of the three book peddlers who had served as prosecution witnesses against the libertine poet Théophile de Viau (whose pernicious influence was violently denounced by the Jesuit priest Garasse), one, Antoine Vitré, became printer to the French clergy, another, Billaine, became bookseller to the Benedictines, and the third, Rocollet, became the personal bookseller of Chancellor Séguier, a figure who for a long time was connected with the ultramontane clan. In reality, the libertine intellectuals displayed extreme caution. As René Pintard has shown,[14] those of Paris openly expressed the greatest reverence toward the Church, and as good disciples of Machiavelli and loyal servants of the king and his first minister, they supported the policies of a France at war with the very Catholic Spain. They were careful to express themselves only with the greatest reserve and avoided the publication of any work that could be prosecuted.

Despite all this, we should not forget that European presses still published many other works. In particular, these included works on law and medicine as well as classical texts, at a time when the humanistic ideal remained the model. They also published an increasing number of historical books that often exemplified new currents of thought, about which I shall speak later. However, above all else, this period witnessed the development of Baroque poetry and the appearance of some of the greatest masterpieces of European literature. Almost everywhere, in Spain and England, and subsequently in France, theatrical troupes increased in number. Thus, Shakespeare (1564–1616) produced *Hamlet* in 1602, *Othello* in 1604, *King Lear* in

1605–7, and *Macbeth* in 1606. Lope de Vega (1562–1635) wrote nearly 1,800 plays, and Tirso de Molina in 1630 published *El Burlador de Sevilla,* the original version of *Don Juan.* The same phenomenon soon appeared in France leading up to the publication of the *Cid* by Pierre Corneille in 1637. The literature of the romance and novel also attained its Golden Age. The pastoral romance, born with the *Diana* of Montemayor (1520–61), conquered Europe and inspired in France the *Astrée* of Honoré d'Urfé, of which the first volume appeared in 1607. Elsewhere, beginning in 1554, Diego de Mendoza published his *Lazarillo de Tormes,* and in 1599 Mateo Alemán's *Guzman de Alfarache,* followed in 1626 by Quevedo's *El Buscòn,* gave new impetus to the picaresque novel, just as Cervantes with his immortal *Don Quixote* (1605–15) sounded the death knell for the medieval chivalric romance. In France, again, the genre of the picaresque novel inspired Sorel's *Francion* (1623) as well as Scarron's *Roman comique* (1651). In 1668, with the *Simplicissimus* of Grimmelhausen, this genre reached Germany, devastated by war. Finally, the heroic novel blossomed in France with Madeleine de Scudéry's *Artamène ou le Grand Cyrus* and *Clélie* of which the first of ten volumes appeared in 1654.

It is striking, therefore, to see how modes and themes, especially those originating in Italy and Spain, were adopted by one country after another by means of translations, or even by the reading of these masterpieces in their original language. Certainly, the great works of Spanish profane literature penetrated into France, notably via the book fairs of Saint-Germain-des-Prés, near Paris.[15] However, literary publications in vernacular languages remained the affair of small groups of specialized booksellers, and the theater, like the romance and novel, was for a long time scorned by the learned who stubbornly yearned for poetry, especially epic poetry.

UNTIL THE DECADE 1620–30, the commerce surrounding the printed book continued because the product stimulated a steady increase in demand. Almost everywhere, the number of presses seemed to increase. However, in 1617, religious war had broken out again in Germany. For thirty years, the Germanic countries would be the principal theater of conflict between the great powers. They would come out of this war devastated for a long time to come. In addition, in 1630 a terrible plague spread throughout Europe, destroying a large part of the population of cities such as Lyon, where book production dwindled. Finally, the religious convents and the libraries of princes and magistrates became progressively saturated with the growing number of large editions. From then on, the publishers in the principal centers engaged in a war in which they systematically produced counterfeit editions with the goal of ruining their competitors and seizing control of those specialized areas for which there was still a market.

Thus, an era of rapid expansion came to an end, and a period that can justly be called a recession began. Let us look briefly at what occurred in three countries: Germany, England, and France. We shall start with Germany. Examine the map showing the participants in the Frankfurt and Leipzig book fairs in the years 1651–75 (map 3). From the years 1626–50, Venice, Paris, and Lyon no longer played an important role on German soil. Antwerp continued to be prominent for a while longer but also withdrew in about 1660. Soon after, within the devastated Holy Roman Empire, only Leiden, Amsterdam, and to some extent Geneva continued to play a role of some importance, most notably by establishing themselves as importers of French books destined for Central and Eastern Europe.

Much was also happening in England over the course of the century. Universities were never more highly populated than on the eve of the revolt against the Stuarts. However, in the years 1620–30, English booksellers withdrew from the Frankfurt fairs, and statistics based on the books conserved at the British Library and the Bodleian show that a period of remarkable growth in production in the years 1621–60 was followed

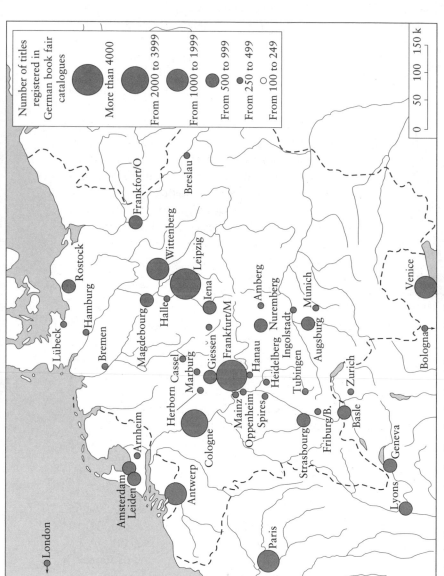

Number of titles
registered in
German book fair
catalogues

More than 4000

From 2000 to 3999

From 1000 to 1999

From 500 to 999

From 250 to 499

From 100 to 249

0   50   100   150 k

London

Amsterdam
Leiden
Arnheim

Antwerp

Paris

Lübeck

Bremen

Hamburg

Rostock

Herborn   Cassel

Cologne

Magdebourg

Halle

Marburg

Giessen

Frankfurt/M

Mainz
Oppenheim
Spires

Strasbourg

Friburg/B.

Basle

Geneva

Lyons

Frankfort/O

Breslau

Wittenberg

Leipzig

Iena

Amberg

Hanau
Heidelberg   Nuremberg
Ingolstadt
Tubingen   Augsburg

Munich

Zurich

Venice

Bologna

Map 3. European booksellers in the Frankfurt and Leipzig fairs, 1651–75

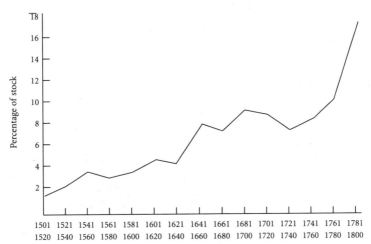

Graph 1. Distribution of "O" books (books catalogued under "O" at the British Library, Bodleian, ULC, etc.)

by a period of relative stagnation that lasted until 1721–40 (graph 1).

Turning to France, we see in the statistics of the number of titles published that I compiled some years ago, based on the collections of the Bibliothèque Nationale, that Parisian production grew considerably until around 1644–45. Then it was followed by a period of decline, then renewed growth between 1661 and 1671, and finally stagnation once again (graph 2). At the same time, from 1640 onward, shorter and shorter books were printed in smaller and smaller formats. Thus, consistency in the number of titles printed evidently masked an economic crisis that worsened as the century progressed.[16]

Elsewhere, Latin books lost ground to those in the vernacular. Indeed, everywhere the latter won out definitively, first in France, then in England, and finally in Germany (graphs 3, 4, and 5). Thus, toward the middle of the seventeenth century, a unique form of culture was in decline, one that represented an erudite form of humanism based on a knowledge of Latin,

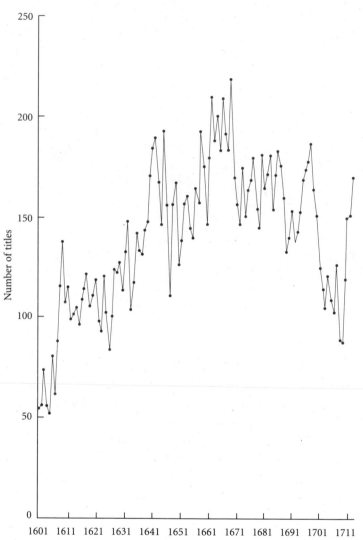

Graph 2. Distribution by titles of French books, 1601–1715

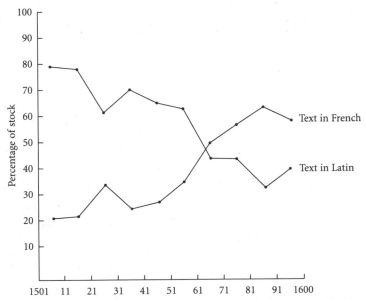

Graph 3. Distribution by language of French and Latin printed books of the sixteenth century

on the study and knowledge of pagan and Christian antiquity, on a cult of tradition, and on the respect for precedent that the Catholic Reformation had in a way reinforced throughout much of Europe.

European culture developed in this manner only because behind an apparently immobile facade everything had been changing. Since 1550, a growing number of travel narratives augmented an awareness of the existence of societies that were not Christian. In addition (and this is essential), the growth of cartography taught a new way of looking at the world by means of the printed page. Moreover, as early as 1620, Bacon proclaimed the need for renovating ancient physics, in 1623 Galileo declared that nature is written in mathematical language, and in 1637 Descartes offered his vindication of

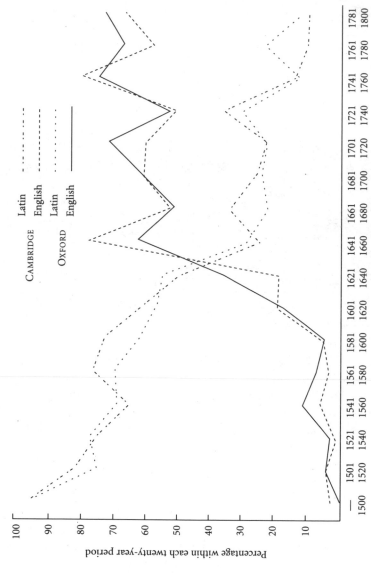

CAMBRIDGE { Latin
              English
OXFORD   { Latin
              English

Percentage within each twenty-year period

100
90
80
70
60
50
40
30
20
10

1501 1521 1541 1561 1581 1601 1621 1641 1661 1681 1701 1721 1741 1761 1781
1500 1520 1540 1560 1580 1600 1620 1640 1660 1680 1700 1720 1740 1760 1780 1800

Graph 4. Distribution by language and date of "O" books in college and departmental libraries

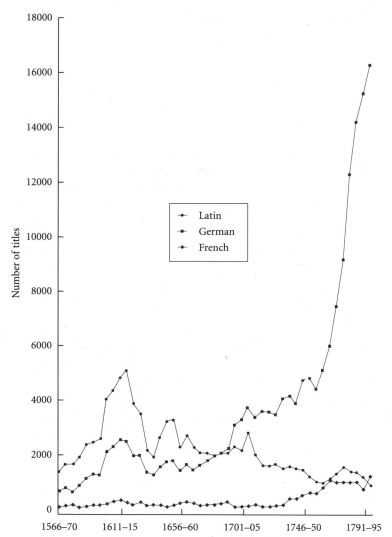

Graph 5. Distribution by language of the books printed in Germany in the German bookfair catalogs

logic. Almost everywhere in Europe, scholars increasingly corresponded with each other. These exchanges in France centered around Nicholas Fabri de Peiresc, magistrate in the parlement of Aix-en-Provence who was responsible for engraving the first map of the moon, and Martin Mersenne, the Capuchin friar and friend of Descartes whose small studio on the Place Royale in Paris became the meeting place of the learned. In addition, mathematics came to be viewed as a useful science, whether for constructing dikes in Holland or for conducting siege warfare. Officers of the Royal Army stationed in Paris between campaigns often took an interest in the challenges that mathematicians liked to present in the form of printed broadsides.

In these circumstances, the placement of Copernicus's *De revolutionibus orbium* on the Index *donec corrigatur* and the condemnation of Galileo in 1633 were only two rearguard battles.[17] Certainly, these actions forced scholars to be prudent and prevented Descartes from publishing his great treatise *De mundo.* But already a page had turned. The burgeoning number of small books written in the vernacular were often, in the middle of the century, entitled *Abrégé, Moyen court* (shortcut), or *Méthode facile,* and, if one thinks about it, the *Discours de la méthode* was really one of them. The necessity for printers and booksellers to innovate in order to survive spawned the sudden appearance of a new type of literature and with it the birth of a new type of author who was referred to by the relatively new term, the *écrivain.*[18] As a result, in 1664, Sorel, an author of many kinds of works, could publish a *Bibliothèque française* in which he happily declared that the great classics of antiquity would henceforth appear in translation and that all subjects would now be treated in the French language. Sorel's work was a bibliography that gives us a picture of the type of works that made up the education of the upright layman, the successor to the humanist scholar.

However, such progress had to have its negative side. This period was one of all sorts of cultural divisions. From this time

on, books circulated within large linguistic regions as if in a
closed circuit, and each nation lived as though in a different
time period. Points of view diverged, lasting divisions occurred.
While Germany temporarily disappeared from the scene, England lived through a revolution. As early as 1644 Milton in
his *Areopagitica* called for freedom of the press. Then, in 1649,
Charles I was executed to the horror of other nations, and this
occurred precisely as the Fronde was brewing in France. But
the latter would be only an aborted revolt. As a consequence, a
prepublication censorship haphazardly introduced in France by
Richelieu became a given. The way was then open for the triumph of absolutism as well as for the blossoming of its cultural
corollary, "classicism." But its hour of glory, corresponding to
the first part of the personal reign of Louis XIV, would not be
without its counterforces and repercussions, as we shall see in
subsequent chapters.

CHAPTER 2

Absolutism and Classicism

From the beginning of the sixteenth century and culminating in the seventeenth century, the French monarchy felt obliged to follow a purposeful cultural policy. In so doing, it made the French language an instrument of its policy of centralization, and little by little it was led to seek to control publishing both because of its concern for maintaining public order and because of its aim of controlling religious and intellectual life. Thus the kings initiated a number of measures that contributed greatly to explaining the development of classicism.

THE CULTURAL POLICY OF THE KINGS of France has never been studied. Its first official expression came when Charles V established a library of vernacular literature including translations of Latin texts deemed of use to the prince.[1] This occurred precisely when the secretaries of the French chancellery came into contact with their homologues at the pontifical court and the chancellery of Florence, the founders of the humanist movement. At that time, a humanism à la française would have developed had the insanity of Charles VI and the misfortunes of France not put an end to this first attempt. An effort was made again at the beginning of the sixteenth century by Louis XII, who established at Blois a library replete with deluxe manuscripts,[2] and subsequently by François I, who had the distinction of being the first king to define a coherent national cultural policy. In order to understand what followed, keep in mind that the royal court was populated by both aristocrats who had received the traditional upbringing of men of the sword and many men of letters who participated actively in the government. Foremost among the latter were the notaries and secretaries of the king, the successors to the men who had been won over to humanism at the end of the fifteenth century. Coming for the most part from the great families of royal officials, their principal role was to formulate and draft the acts originating in the chancellery, and they were often destined for brilliant political careers. Grolier, the illustrious bibliophile, was in his youth notary and secretary to the king, as was Guillaume Budé whose grandfather and father had held the charge of *grand audiencier* of the chancellery, the most important post after those of chancellor and keeper of the king's charters.[3]

At the beginning of the reign of François I, many of these men had been close to Marguerite de Navarre, the king's sister, and to the *Evangelistes* in the circle of the great Briçonnet family. Thus was established a veritable humanist lobby in which Guillaume Budé, who from 1519 had a brilliant administrative career, took the lead. In 1520 or 1522 this lobby was able to obtain the creation of a new library installed in the château of Fontainebleau above the famous gallery that celebrated the king's greatness.[4] In accordance with the ideal of the Renaissance, the Latin and especially Greek manuscripts that scholars needed for their work were assembled there. Then between 1529 and 1534, upon his release from captivity following the disaster of Pavia, François I appointed readers of Greek, the Hebraic languages, mathematics, and Latin eloquence who were beholden only to him. Thus, the College of Royal Readers, today known as the Collège de France, was born, and it has remained strictly independent from university affairs ever since. Subsequently a number of humanist printers, including the well-known Robert Estienne, were named Printers to the King.[5] Among their prerogatives was that, should the need arise, they were able to sidestep the ordinary courts and appeal directly to their sovereign. Finally, in 1539–40, François I had created at his personal expense the Greek characters deemed essential for scholarship.[6] The punches for these, engraved by Garamond, are preserved today at the Imprimerie Nationale in Paris after having long served in the sixteenth and seventeenth centuries for the publication of an incredible number of classical Greek, Byzantine, and patristic texts. Royal support for humanism was not a question of patronage in the narrow sense of the term but of a policy aimed at encouraging a current of moderate reformist thought at a time when the Lutheran reform began to tear apart Christianity.

Furthermore, the royal cultural policy did not stop there. We will see in the last chapter that the king encouraged the adoption of Roman type for the printing of books in French in order to proclaim the equality of the national language with ancient Latin, while Gothic script, commonly referred to as *bâtarde,* remained the only type of writing used in the chancellery, the royal administration, and the courts. I will also show how Robert Estienne, a protégé of the king, undertook the fabrication of the accents and diacritical marks still in use in France today. Estienne issued a *Traicté de la grammaire française* in the preface to which he invoked the usage of "the most learned in our language who throughout their lives have frequented the royal court of France, and the Parlement, as well as the chancellery and the chambre des comptes, where the language is written and pronounced in its purest form."[7] Here we have a policy aimed at forming a national language in a realm still divided into multiple dialects. This policy found its culmination and raison d'être in the Royal Ordonnance of Villers-Cotteret of 1539. Article III of this act prescribed that all judicial documents must be pronounced, recorded, and delivered to all parties in the "mother tongue of France" in order henceforth to avoid the inherent ambiguity in Latin words.[8] Thus, the moment had arrived when Joachim du Bellay, who, it must be remembered, belonged to a family close to the king, would publish in 1549 (new style 1550) his *Defense et illustration de la langue française*.

Meanwhile, the Royal attitude vis-à-vis the book trades gradually began to change for religious and political reasons as well as for economic ones. The system of privilèges evolved in response to economic conditions. Since the end of the fifteenth and the beginning of the sixteenth century, booksellers and printers, who had invested considerable sums to publish expensive works, began to realize that there was nothing to prevent others from printing less expensive counterfeit editions of the same texts. They therefore began the practice of requesting the royal authorities to grant them a privilège, or license, a sort of temporary monopoly for a given book. For a long time, these licenses were awarded not only by the royal chancellery but also by the parlements and secondary courts without anyone raising objections.[9]

At the same time, during this century of the Reformation, the royal authority above all felt obliged to intervene in the affairs of booksellers for religious reasons. From the years 1520 to 1530 and after, ecclesiastical and lay authorities both deemed it necessary to prohibit books of Protestant propaganda and attempted to ensure that new books would not be published without their permission. Here again the monarchy granted permissions on various levels, but it still did not succeed in reducing the publication of "bad books."[10]

France's political situation worsened after the death of Henri

II (1559). A vacillating royal authority that proved itself incapable of preventing the propaganda emanating from various factions succeeded even less in establishing the groundwork for new legislation concerning censorship and the practices of booksellers, even though the partisans of these laws laid the ideological foundation for the absolutism that would triumph in the next century.

The principal motive behind the monarchy's legislation in the area of censorship was that royal officials felt it necessary to react to decisions taken at the end of the Council of Trent. At Trent (as we have seen earlier), the Catholic Church claimed for itself the right to impose an Index of forbidden books and thereby to survey directly printers and booksellers. Following the example of the policy of the king of Spain,[11] the king of France by virtue of the Ordonnance of Moulins (1566) established that henceforth all new books had to be provided with licenses bearing the great seal.[12] By this, it is clear that the monarchy intended to control the publication of new books. Authors and editors would have to submit manuscripts to the chancellery in return for receiving not only permission to print, but also a copyright whose duration depended on the particular work and the government's good will.

But who would evaluate the manuscripts of new books? It seems that the government envisioned that the task would be entrusted to the mâitres des requêtes de l'hôtel. But the crown forgot to take into consideration the faculty of theology. This body, which the weakened king could ill afford to offend, believed that its learned members, and not royal agents, had the right of censorship. As a result the royal plan could not be put into practice.

It must also be remembered that at this time the papacy was engaged in an ambitious program of correcting holy texts and standardizing liturgical books so as to make them conform solely to the Roman rite. It clearly intended to control the printing of these texts throughout the Christian world in order to avoid corruptions stemming either from contact with heretical thought or from persisting loyalty to local liturgical traditions. Pontifical and royal authorities first agreed to grant extensive monopolies over sacred texts to booksellers such as Jacques Kerver in Paris (1564) and Guillaume Rouillé in Lyon (1572). Later, following a period of disputes and trials, the king granted in 1586 to the Compagnie des Usages, an essentially Parisian association of large booksellers, a limited monopoly that superseded earlier pontifical privilèges. At the same time, another association, the Compagnie du Navire, received a monopoly for publishing the texts of the Church fathers.[13]

The monarchy during the same period was also forced to intervene increasingly in the organization of the book trades in order to maintain public order. On two occasions, first in 1539–42 and then in 1571–72, the journeymen printers revolted against their masters because they imposed harsh quotas and working conditions. The journeymen unleashed strikes that today's French historians of labor movements consider to be the first example of modern work stoppages. Forced to react, the crown instituted the first regulations that in the beginning of the seventeenth century would lead to the establishment of the Corporation of Parisian Printers, Booksellers, and Binders, which was endowed with statutes in 1618, and whose officers were henceforth charged with maintaining order in the book trades.[14]

To summarize, at the end of the Wars of Religion, the monarchy had demonstrated that it was unable to control the publication of new books. However, it had succeeded in creating powerful corporations, entities possessing considerable monopolies, in spite of the tenacious resistance of the Parlement. Henceforth, the monarchy found itself confronting the official representatives of the Parisian book trade in the persons of the Syndic and his assistants of the Community of Parisian Printers, Booksellers, and Binders, and their provincial counterparts. It thus disposed of a new network for exerting pressure that would be utilized in the seventeenth century to create what one would be tempted to call typographical absolutism. Moreover, royal propaganda of a new variety began to appear. For a long time, the king's glory had manifested itself principally in parades and public ceremonies—notably royal entrances that were commemorated modestly by printed booklets. However, the challenge to royal authority by Protestant protagonists, and especially by those of the Catholic Ligue, had stimulated among believers in a strong king, those known as the politiques, the rise of a renewed monarchical ideology. Therefore, learned royalists gradually led an effort to elaborate new theories of royal power. One of my students, Jean-Marc Chatelain, has shown, in a dissertation as yet unpublished, how a monarchical culture of glory developed among the educated.[15] This culture, based on antique and Christian traditions, became politically more significant as the person of the king became the chief focus of hostility during the second part of the reign of Henri IV. Thus began a form of propaganda that was exemplified by the images often included in the collections of coats of arms and emblems that continued to be printed throughout the reign of Louis XIII. This genre reached its fullest development in the beginning of the personal reign of Louis XIV. Finally, beginning in 1550, studies concerning the history of France, its relics, and its monuments developed in a parallel manner and for the same reasons. Kings, anxious to encourage this movement, created at least as early as the end of the reign of Henri II the office of royal historiographer.[16] It is hardly surprising that this policy was systematically developed during the period of the Wars of Religion when royal power and sometimes even the person of the king were the objects of numerous attacks. To defend royal authority, the office of historiographer of France was created during the reign of Charles IX, and the first incumbent was Bernard de Girard de Haillan. As time passed, alongside the historiographer of France several royal historiographers appeared. This, however, is a subject about which I dare not write in great length in view of the works of Professor Orest Ranum, lest I give the impression, as one says in France, of attempting to teach Latin to the priest.[17]

WE HAVE SEEN IN CHAPTER I that the Catholic Reformation greatly encouraged the progress of printing, publishing, and bookselling at least until 1630–35. In addition, in a France convalescing after the Wars of Religion, French literature experienced a brilliant renewal, and the number of books grew unrelentingly.

In a period in which the economic conditions were less and less favorable, it is understandable that the French book trades attracted a constantly growing number of newcomers. From the beginning of the century, in effect, many of the youngest sons of provincial families of modest means, without a future where they were, came to Paris to seek their fortune. There they attempted to subsist by selling books and pamphlets, a phenomenon that has repeated itself again and again. As our *Histoire de l'édition française* has shown, the Parisian book world has always renewed itself in this manner, and many of today's large publishing houses originated in just this fashion.[18] Nonetheless, it is equally true that the number of small typographic shops increased more than the demand for them and that innumerable "disreputable" persons, who congregated on the Pont Neuf, joined the authorized peddlers whose principal task was to hawk official documents.

This influx of newcomers quickly encouraged the appearance of a growing number of leaflets and pamphlets of all sorts. The earlier records of pamphlet publication set by the Ligue[19] in the preceding century were surpassed in large measure during such political crises as the meeting of the Estates General in 1614, the assassination of Concini, and the struggle in midcentury between the Queen Mother Marie de Médicis and the entourage of her son.[20] The *Journal* of Pierre de L'Estoile, an unrepentant collector, instructs us on what this literature was like. However, let us not be misled. As can be seen in the dialogues of the *Caquets de l'accouchée,* the pamphlets as well as the majority of leaflets were destined for an elite ranging from presidents of the court and pharmacists to lawyers and doctors.[21] The rest of the population, from the merchant to the modest wage earner, were content either to read broadsides or to hear them read aloud and to examine propagandist engravings accompanied by short texts. This is not at all to say that the masses were uninterested in political events, but only that their sources of information were generally oral and secondhand—a subject to which I shall return.

In broad outline, such was the situation when Richelieu advanced to become first minister. His personality had such an impact on the history of France's cultural institutions that I must pause here for a moment. A prince garbed in a crimson robe, cardinal of the Counter-Reformation, he simultaneously united in his person, in the words of Marc Fumaroli, "the *virtu* of a Machiavellian ruler, the masterful authority of a prince of the post-Trent Church, and the ability to change rapidly both word and deed that characterized the *uomo universale* of the Renaissance; he thereby raised politics to the level of a major art." He was a writer on almost every subject. When he was still only bishop of Luzon, he was particularly noted for his work on theology and dogmatic controversies. When he wished to influence public opinion after his rise to power, he personally directed a team of pamphleteers. He engaged in political, diplomatic, and military activities on a European scale with the aim of achieving for himself the glory of a founding hero.[22] He contemplated writing a great history of his ministry and therefore increased the number of historiographers and requested them to furnish him with the requisite documentation. Priding himself on his unusual talents, he assembled a personal academy that he intended to function according to his instructions. Finally, to reach these many goals and envisaging that all literary activity would center around his own person, he brought together in his palace a considerable collection of books, thereby constituting a very important library. Such a person would naturally wish to control very closely the printing press, which constituted both the principal medium for either criticizing or justifying his policies and the potential tool for proclaiming his glory.

With the aforementioned in mind, remember that the day after the *Journée des Dupes,* Richelieu decided to support the creation of the first French periodical by granting to a doctor from Montpellier (whom he knew very well and who had already established a place in history as the inventor of the classified ad) the exclusive right of publishing a weekly newspaper, the *Gazette,* in which the king and even Richelieu himself did not hesitate to publish articles. The recent research of Gilles Feyel has brought to light the origins of this publication and has shown that its success was reflected very quickly in numerous provincial reprintings.[23] However, the monopoly granted by the monarchy for publishing periodicals soon elicited considerable protest, and by the end of the reign of Louis XV it had encouraged the rise of an opposition press located beyond the frontiers of France. In the course of the eighteenth century an increasingly intolerable situation existed, one frequently denounced on the eve of the Revolution.

Scarcely installed in his post, Richelieu tried to establish a royal right to prepublication censorship. His first problem in this regard was to find trusted men to examine the manuscripts of new books. To this end in 1624 the cardinal sought to entrust the task of censorship to four doctors of theology to be chosen as permanent official censors. This measure, which deprived authors of the right to choose their own censors, immediately ran into the opposition of the Faculty of Theology, which held that in principle each of its members had the right to grant approvals for publications. The cardinal was thus forced to renounce his plan and to institute instead the now famous Ordonnance of 1629, the *Code Michaud* (from the name of the garde des sceaux Michel de Marillac). In article 52 it stated that henceforth it would no longer be the persons requesting a license but the chancellor himself who would designate the experts to examine new books.

With his authority now affirmed, Richelieu could once again address the issue using as his agent Chancellor Séguier, appointed in 1633. Séguier immediately established himself as a specialist in affairs concerning the press. Starting in 1634, he closely oversaw the granting of printing rights for which he instituted a special register, and he began the practice of naming book censors orally in order to cut short all protest. Quite naturally, he then gave the right of examining manuscripts submitted to him to the royal notaries and secretaries who already had the task of preparing the text of the licenses. Nevertheless, he reserved to himself the right to intercede personally in difficult cases. So it was that the first royal censors were people like Conrart, who signed an enormous number of licenses, and the mathematician Beaugendre. Descartes hardly appreciated this system, for it forced him to publish his *Discours de la méthode* in Holland.[24]

Thus, prepublication censorship became a reality in France precisely when publishing was experiencing a crisis of overproduction, aggravated by the slump in sales of scholarly works. Publishers were increasing the number of new books just to survive. Realizing that the orthodoxy of new publications was linked to the health of the publishing industry, Richelieu undertook to reorganize the Compagnie des Usages and the Compagnie du Navire despite the resistance of the Parlement, traditionally hostile to this sort of monopoly. Favoring excessively Parisians to whom he was more closely linked, he designated as leaders of these companies a small group of trusted men at the head of whom he placed his personal bookseller, Sébastien Cramoisy. Cramoisy's loyalty was unquestioned, and he had additional advantages. He belonged to a Ligue family and thus enjoyed the complete confidence of Pope Urban VIII, his nephews the Cardinals Barberini, as well as the Jesuits. Richelieu granted numerous privilèges for republishing reputable old books and divided them among the publishers who were favorably viewed by the monarchy. In addition, he took great care that the "manna" of official government publications was reserved only for carefully chosen royal printers. Thus we may conclude that in publishing as well as in other areas the Cardinal-Minister meant to rely only on groups of loyal servants.

All this, however, was still not sufficient for Richelieu. He regarded with envy the Plantin-Moretus Press that in Antwerp, a Spanish territory, was producing superb editions containing frontispieces designed by Rubens. He surely was sorry to see the same shop publish sumptuous works that included pamphlets glorifying his former protectress, Marie de Médicis, who, having taken refuge in Belgium, had become his most tenacious adversary. Certainly he regretted that Blaeu and Elzevir in Amsterdam and Leiden were producing high-quality editions at a time when the best French presses were manufacturing only a mediocre product.

This situation incited Richelieu to instruct Sublet de Noyers to create the Imprimerie Royale to compete with these foreign establishments. It was magnificently housed in the gallery of the Louvre. As always, the first question was how to finance such an enterprise. For example, it was envisioned that the new establishment would have a monopoly over the publishing of Greek, Latin, and French dictionaries and lexicons, the Bible, the *Corpus juris civilis,* and the works of Thomas Aquinas, in a word, the principal "best sellers" of the age. But in the end this plan was rejected out of fear of spreading discontent among Parisian printers. Instead, the new royal printing house headed by the intrepid Sébastien Cramoisy had to be content with publishing sumptuous works destined for distribution by the king. The new press began by publishing, in addition to the New Testament and the complete Bible, a selection of the most celebrated texts of the Catholic Reformation including the *Spiritual Exercises* of Ignatius de Loyola, the *Introduction à la vie dévote* of François de Sales, and the *De imitatione Christi*. Richelieu's own theological treatises and the *Poemata* of a certain Matteo Barberini—none other than Pope Urban VIII—were of course also included. A few other well-known texts, such as the collected works of Horace and Virgil, were printed as well. Taken together, these titles constituted a veritable library of deluxe volumes produced in folio format with copperplate engraved frontispieces.[25]

However, Richelieu's most prestigious contribution to the field of letters was his creation of the Académie Française. To understand its significance, we must understand the intellectual and literary life of Richelieu's time. On the one hand, the intellectual heirs of the humanism of Erasmus—royal magistrates and officials, university scholars in Protestant countries, monks and friars in Catholic countries, and librarians as well—in their desire to lead men of government along the path toward wisdom sometimes pursued scientific research in an age when the physical sciences and mathematics were coming under the influence of what is commonly called the mechanical revolution. In Paris the groups that made up the *Respublica litteraria* were represented in particular by the "erudite libertines," who came together in the quarters of the Dupuy brothers, keepers of the Royal Library, authors of treatises on the Gallican liberties and the reign of Philip the Fair, and cousins of the de Thou family. Equally representative of the *Respublica litteraria* were the scholars who met in the cell of Father Mersenne in the convent of the *Minimes* located on the Place Royale. The learned kept their distance from politics, and, as a group, they were highly respected and often independent-minded individuals.[26]

On the other hand, there were those who, as Alain Viala has reminded us,[27] would soon come to be known as *écrivains*. In order to understand what these persons represented for our period we must for a moment go back in time. If the Pléiade poets may be considered court poets, then the new generation of poets that appeared at the beginning of the seventeenth century may be labeled baroque poets. Of the latter, Théophile de Viau and Tristan L'Hermite were the notable examples. In this same milieu, another school of poetry also developed, of whom the most influential figure was Malherbe. Malherbe was the official court poet, indeed its panegyrist, who placed perfection of form above creativity. However, all these individuals had to earn a living. True to ancient tradition, they placed themselves in the service of important personages for whom they were obliged to compose amorous letters as well as political statements. Existing as clients of the powerful, they were always in search of patrons who might offer remuneration by supporting their work. Without question they played an important role during the conflicts that followed the assassination of Henri IV by composing some of the growing number of pamphlets.

Another aspect of these *écrivains* was that, after about 1620, they began the practice of gathering in private academies to converse about literature and to attempt to establish literary norms. Indeed, the number of these individuals increased dramatically in proportion to the efforts of publishers to increase the number of new titles in the French language. From this time on, the rules of the game evolved to the point where some *écrivains* adopted relatively new strategies and sought to establish careers no longer by winning the esteem of scholars, but by addressing the public directly in the hope both of having their works performed in the theaters and especially of increasing the sale of their books. At the same time, many of these *écrivains* supplemented their incomes, or indeed tried to make their living, by demanding money from their publisher, as did, for example, Corneille and Scarron.

Richelieu's literary tastes and political preoccupations naturally encouraged him to favor these new scholars who were more malleable than traditional men of letters and therefore more apt to play the role of unconditional panegyrists. The rest of this story is well known. Richelieu heard from Boisrobert about meetings being held at the home of the young Huguenot

Valentin Conrart, a notary and secretary of the king who had the responsibility of composing the printing licenses granted to men of letters. The cardinal then decided to bring together a group of *écrivains* carefully chosen from the circles of the leading patrons of the period into an Académie and to include a number of the leading personalities among them. Thus was born the official system of the Académie, which did not take long to develop into an instrument first of literary and subsequently of scientific and artistic approval as well. By the beginning of the eighteenth century it had evolved into a veritable intellectual grid that extended across France to the great benefit of Parisian centralism.[28]

The creating of the Académie just when the monarchy was developing a system of prepublication censorship colors it, in reality, with a certain measure of ambiguity. It is reasonable to consider whether the cardinal, then at the height of his power, hoped to find in this body a corps of censors. Given the orientation of most of the Academicians one might even wonder if Richelieu's intention was not to impose official norms on the actual composition of works as the Académie actually tried to do during the controversy over the *Cid*. However, the Parlement prevented such a course by agreeing to register the Académie's statutes only when its activity was limited to the examination of manuscripts submitted voluntarily. The statutes as adopted also envisioned that the Académie would prepare a *Rhetoric* and a *Poetics* as well as a dictionary of the French language. The first two projects were abandoned, but that of a periodically revised dictionary still constitutes the principal task of today's Academicians.

Make no mistake about it, however: the Académie performed an essential function in an absolutist state. It played an official role as panegyrist for the king and his first minister, but its principal mission was to provide the Augustan age that France enjoyed thanks to the cardinal with a language that had the universality and durability of Ciceronian Latin. This is a project reminiscent of that outlined by Robert Estienne a century earlier. Indeed, Vaugelas in the preface of his *Remarques sur la langue française* laid the groundwork for the *Dictionnaire* by declaring that its content was to be based on *bel usage,* that is, "the manner of speaking of the sounder portion of the court consistent with the style of the best writers." Such a double canon of authority demonstrates that the Académie was never conceived to be a mere association of grammarians.[29]

Richelieu, however, does not seem to have viewed the institution that he created as a final end. Private remarks that he made toward the end of his life indicate that he was thinking about creating for the "belles sciences" (i.e., the belles lettres) a *grand collège* "that would make use of all that was most dazzling in European literature." The Academicians were envisaged as the directors of this new institution. One can imagine that in this context the Imprimerie Royale had been but the first step in the cardinal's plan to control printing more and more closely, indeed, to make the art of printing a state industry. As we shall see, however, here his plans took into account neither the book trade nor public opinion.

BY TAKING THE MEASURES that I have just enumerated, had Cardinal Richlieu lost touch with reality? Didn't he realize that during his ministry the Parisian book world had developed in an anarchical fashion and that it was experiencing an increasingly acute crisis of overproduction? The number of printing establishments, publishers, and bookstands continued to increase, creating an altogether intolerable situation. So bad were matters that, beginning in 1639, the monarchy finally became conscious of events and reacted by electing reliable men in whom they had complete confidence to head the office of the Community of Parisian Printers, Booksellers, and Binders. But this did not please everyone, and the carriage taking the Lieutenant Civil and the Procureur du Châtelet to the polling place was stoned. For a detailed discussion of the quarrels dividing the community, I refer you to my previous work.[30] Suffice it to say here that the community was soon divided between two opposing syndics.

This was the situation when Richelieu died (December 1642), followed shortly thereafter by Louis XIII (May 1643). The heir to the cardinal's views on these matters, Chancellor Séguier, who had already suppressed so many revolts, took the responsibility of naming a new group of officers to head the recalcitrant community. The dominant figure of this group was Sébastien Cramoisy (*Arrêt du Conseil* of 2 October 1643).

Cramoisy immediately set to work taking a census of Parisian printing establishments, noting in each instance the number of presses, journeymen, and apprentices. His findings were astonishing. Sixteen printing shops out of seventy possessed only a single press, a violation of the regulations, and only 80 presses out of a total of 183 operated on a regular basis; the others "awaited requests for *factums,* decrees, discourses, satires, songs and other leaflets." In the face of this situation, Chancellor Séguier and his advisors seem to have envisioned taking a drastic measure: "To place all the presses in one or several collèges in eight large rooms approximately 75 feet long by 37 feet wide or in sixteen rooms divided in half. In each, they would place ten presses, five on each side with their type cases set before windows, correcting tables, etc." However, Cramoisy had no difficulty in pointing out the inanity of such a measure since it would have been practically unenforceable, and he reminded the Chancellor that since the regents of the collèges would themselves be authors of a large number of pamphlets, it would be inadvisable to lodge the printers in colleges under their supervision. Instead, he suggested eliminating those printing shops operating only a single press and regrouping the rest into fifty major workshops.[31]

These severe measures were intended to try to regain control of a situation that was increasingly grave. One must remember that the *Augustinus* of Jansenius, published at Louvain in 1640,

47

was reprinted at Paris as early as 1641. Immediately, the theological world was incensed to the delight of Parisian printers, who saw an inundation of pamphlets as well as weighty treatises enter their shops. Richelieu detested Jansenius, the presumed author of a pamphlet entitled *Mars Gallicus* that had severely attacked him. The cardinal, who was very wary of theological quarrels, tried to react. However, after his death, the quarrel exploded, especially after Antoine Arnauld published his *Traité de la fréquente communion*. Under these conditions, and confronted by a weakened monarchy, the world of the rue Saint-Jacques could no longer be restrained, and it multiplied the number of new works either favorable or hostile to the new doctrine, usually, of course, without asking for the authorization of the chancellor. The result was that the feverish year of 1644 broke all records in the number of titles published.

Unfortunately for the printers, all fevers decline, and once again, beginning in 1647–48, they had to search for new works to publish. The Fronde arrived just in time to answer their need. I do not intend to devote too much time here to the role that the press played in this revolt, or rather, this series of revolts. I shall refer you to Hubert Carrier's monumental study on the Mazarinades and limit myself to underlining several points relevant to my theme.

The first concerns the role played by the publishing offices created by the great princes. Their activities clearly demonstrate the danger of allowing *écrivains* to attach themselves to the circles of their patrons, and as Hubert Carrier has demonstrated, this is especially true for the most well-known authors who did not hesitate to write pamphlets. In the same fashion, the most well-connected publishers were quick to promote the views of their most important clients. The result was the development of a system of disseminating propaganda reminiscent of that of the Ligue. Finally, based on an examination of the pamphlets and their diffusion, Carrier concluded that certain pamphlets, in particular broadsides, reached the population, at least in Paris, and that, in certain phases, the Fronde was truly a popular movement.³²

It is also not my intention here to explain why this revolt finally failed. However, it is relevant to my topic to underline the important consequences of its defeat. Certainly Cardinal Mazarin did not take any serious measures of reprisal in the years following the Fronde, and never during the period of the ancien régime had the press been more free. While it is true that the Jansenist fever was rekindled in certain circles at the time of the publication of the *Lettres provinciales,* I have shown that this clandestine pamphlet continued to be published only as long as Fouquet felt free to continue to pick a quarrel with Chancellor Séguier.³³ When the time was appropriate, Fouquet knew how to stop the whole affair by using his brother as an intermediary. In fact, after the Fronde the climate changed completely. The opposition of many of the great princes had diminished, and henceforth the writings and engravings intended to glorify the queen mother and the infant-king multiplied, portending a glorious reign. In a word, everyone was awaiting the arrival of the Master.

THE AGE OF LOUIS XIV was a consequence of that which preceded it. Louis XIV was obviously a Renaissance prince. The most enduring image we have of him is undoubtedly the engraving that represents him astride a horse, dressed as a Roman emperor at the head of a troop of princes of the blood at the time of the celebrations of the birth of the dauphin. This prince did not like books, and it is doubtful that he read much. On the contrary, he liked to surround himself with old manuscripts, drawings, medals, and precious objects. He viewed his cabinet des antiques at Versailles as the core of his treasury.³⁴ Not far from there, his personal library was made up of calligraphic manuscripts commemorating, in particular, the celebrations given in his honor. For him, literature was above all oral, whether the subject was the theater or panegyric discourse such as Bossuet's funeral orations. But his greatest merit was to have eminently good taste and a certain respect for literary independence. His aesthetics were truly beyond reproach from his subjects.

As the Sun King, he was the center of everything. It is not surprising therefore that Colbert—the agent responsible for overseeing his glorification—periodically selected the best European authors to compose laudatory speeches in exchange for pensions. We should not be deceived into thinking that this well-publicized system amounted to a great enterprise. Because of the modest size of the royal pensions and their relatively limited numbers, the sums expended were small when compared to the money spent before the Fronde by the great princes eager for the services of some of the *écrivains* and when compared to the expenses sustained for the same purposes by ministers such as Richelieu, Séguier, and even the miserly Mazarin.

As we have seen, Richelieu constituted a splendid library where he welcomed the *écrivains* engaged in his service. Séguier and Mazarin did the same. Even though Colbert himself collected rare manuscripts, he first endeavored to develop the collection of his royal master. In order to be able to supervise more closely the king's collection, he installed them in a building located at the back of his own garden. Here readers were welcomed in a large, well-equipped room at one end of which was placed the empty throne of the absent king. He also assigned to the royal library his best librarians, Carcavi and Clément. Applying the principle of good order to the contents of the king's collection, Clément developed a classification system for the royal printed books that today still forms the basis for the classification system used by the Bibliothèque Nationale.[35]

At this time the academic system was expanded by the reorganization of the Academy of Painting and Sculpture in 1664, and the creation of the Academy of Sciences in 1666 and the Academy of Inscriptions in 1663. The precise task of the last body was to compose the inscriptions intended to celebrate the glory of the king on monuments and medals. Finally, the Royal Observatory was inaugurated in 1675. All that remained was to establish the nature of the publications to be issued by the Imprimerie Royale. Colbert's practical mind turned naturally to the sciences and technologies that seemed most promising for the growth of French industry. He proposed that his sovereign utilize the excellent engravers of the French school to publish on large pages depictions of the most recent inventions. However, this idea did not interest the king, for whom the celebration of his own glory was more important. Louis ordered representations of the spectacular fetes that he loved to give and reproductions of the masterpieces decorating his residences.[36]

The Sun King could not in any way be tarnished by disorder. Colbert, always true to himself, thus had to apply the maxim of order to literature and the life of the intellect. He did so with the conscientiousness, rigor, and single-minded purpose characteristic of all his actions. He began by sending his emissaries to Holland to negotiate the suppression of publications that were unflattering to the king and his family such as *Les amours du grand Alcandre* (the implication being the loves of Louis XIV) or *Les amours de Madame*. At the same time, he tried to prohibit "bad books" from entering Paris. By the nomination of a lieutenant of the police, the famous La Reynie, Colbert was able to impose draconian controls at the entrances to the city. Month after month, an enormous quantity of books was confiscated. Anne Sauvy has compiled a list of these works.[37]

However, Colbert knew very well that it was even more important to ensure that the Parisians themselves could no longer publish lampoons and pamphlets. He held forth on this subject in front of the old Séguier during meetings of the Conseil de Police where he proposed that henceforth printers be obliged to use type that bore identifiable marks, as if that were possible! Thereafter he rallied to the solution proposed earlier by Cramoisy, to suppress the small printing shops that were the most compromised. He did not flinch from limiting the number of authorized typographic shops in the capital to thirty-six. This brutal and efficacious policy condemned to ruin the families of those printers whose establishments would be abolished at their death, but it encouraged a necessary consolidation in a period of economic recession. In 1686 Colbert's successors extended this policy to the provinces; it was made more severe again in 1704 and 1739. Although this approach was beneficial as long as the economic crisis lasted, its perverse effects were increasingly felt when Parisian printers became accustomed to charging exorbitant prices for their wares.[38]

However, all this was not sufficient for ministers of the Great King who were ever anxious to control with greater efficacy the production of the presses. They therefore returned to and expanded a policy that had been initially tried a century earlier and that had been expanded more fully by Séguier on the eve of the Fronde. Thus, despite the stubborn resistance of Parlement, Colbert and his successors increasingly prolonged privilèges for those booksellers and printers deemed to be friendly to the king. Such preferential prolongations and the selective granting of new privilèges for old titles soon began to constitute veritable stipends for reliable printers. In exchange, the monarchy sometimes asked for them to publish scholarly works judged to be useful to the public at large.

From around 1661 to 1685, France dominated Europe while resistance to its hegemony was growing, and the king imposed peace among the Catholic factions while hoping for the collapse of Protestantism. During this brief period, everything was anticipated, organized, and normalized in order to stop time, maintain equilibrium, and proclaim the king's glory. A psychology thus existed that permitted literature as a classical art to achieve its apogee, just when the domesticated high nobility possessed great culture and perfect taste. It is not surprising, therefore, that this short period was marked by the greatest masterpieces of classical French literature: the *Précieuses ridicules* of Molière was presented for the first time in 1660, his *École des femmes* in 1661, the *Critique de l'École des femmes* and the *Impromptu de Versailles* in 1662. Molière's *Tartuffe*, like the *Contes* of La Fontaine, dates from 1664. The *Don Juan* of Molière and the *Maximes* of La Rochefoucauld date from 1665, Molière's *Misanthrope* and the *Médecin malgré lui* appeared in 1666. The *Andromaque* of Racine had its debut in 1667; the *Avare* of Molière, the first collection of the *Fables* of La Fontaine, the *Britannicus* of Racine, and the *Lettres de la réligieuse portugaise* all date from 1668. The *Oraison funèbre d'Henriette d'Angleterre* of Bossuet, the *Bourgeois gentilhomme* of Molière, and the *Bérenice* of Racine date from 1670, as well as the *Pensées* of Pascal, published posthumously. In the following years, Mme. de Sévigne wrote her famous *Letters,* Molière presented his *Femmes savantes* and Racine his *Bajazet,* and Cardinal de Retz his *Mémoires* in 1672. The *Malade imaginaire* appeared in 1673, *Phèdre* in 1677, the *Princesse de Cleves* of Mme. de Lafayette in 1678. Bossuet's *Discours sur l'histoire universelle* was published in 1681, Fontenelle's *Pensées diverses sur la Comète* and *Dialogue des morts* in 1682. Bossuet's *Oraison funèbre de la reine Marie-Thérèse* appeared in 1683.

In the year 1685 the situation became unsettled. The revocation of the Edict of Nantes resulted in the flight from France of an entire intellectual elite, the French Protestants, who fled in large numbers to Holland. Among them were many printers and dynamic publishers and booksellers. At the same time, the rules governing publishing, which were so heavily weighted toward the Parisian printers, forced provincial sellers to live in a clandestine world of counterfeit and illicit publications. Thus, while the era of Versailles was coming to a close, a new period was beginning to which I shall return later.

CHAPTER 3

The Reading Public and Its Books

Let us now reverse our approach and turn our attention to the world of the reader. Historians today are very interested, and rightly so, in the ways in which readers receive books and in their reactions when confronted with a particular text. I shall not consider here these aspects of reading. Instead, I would like to show how the world of the reader was organized (I would even be tempted to say structured), how readers adopted certain models, how books circulated, and how the opinion of cultivated individuals, that is, the learned and "upright people" who made up most of the clientele of seventeenth-century booksellers, was shaped. Indeed, all this occurred toward the middle of the seventeenth century, when a new literature that aimed at being clear and reasonable was being accepted in France. Finally, I would like to demonstrate how the elite reading public of France at the end of the century gradually came to hold opinions that conflicted with the established order and how the world of the book was organized to respond to this new challenge.

It is best to begin at the end of the sixteenth century with the development throughout Europe of a network of libraries that are still at the core of today's libraries, that of the Duke of Wolfenbüttel, for example, who was assured a solid cash flow from the mines of Harz mountains, created what was without doubt the most important library of his time. Simultaneously, the University of Leiden established collections that were destined to be famous, and on its model Sir Thomas Bodley founded the library in Oxford that still bears his name.

Unquestionably, princes of this period were, as always, desirous of accumulating ostentatious examples of their wealth, and they therefore wished to mark their reigns with foundations of this type. It is also true that such creations appeared to be indispensable at a time when people began to realize that the printing press had spectacularly increased the number of books, and when it was deemed essential, based on the ideas outlined by Petrarch, to provide scholars with the means to pursue their studies. In Catholic countries, the Roman Church took the lead in this movement. Its chief concern was to constitute centers that would assure its own intellectual superiority in the struggle against Protestantism. This point of view was shared by many Catholic princes and other important personages.

Certainly such implantations were manifestations of an ideology that first became apparent in the decor and reconstructions of the Vatican Library, which served as a model for the entire Catholic world. This ideology was accompanied by the creation of an emblematic universe in which the allegories suggested a well-defined cultural program. This ideology was even evident in the way books were classified and aligned on the shelves, which looked like galleries. There volumes, stamped with their owners' arms, were lined up in an ordering that mirrored a peculiar conception of the universe.

One wonders why, under these conditions, the king's library, repatriated to Paris under Charles IX, remained neglected for so long and was virtually without a fixed location. Whatever the answer may be, it must be remembered that the two great ministers, Richelieu and Mazarin, both collectors interested in promoting their own glory, amassed prestigious libraries. It must also be recalled that Chancellor Séguier was an even more impassioned bibliophile and collector. He brought together in galleries superbly decorated by paintings of Vouet and mosaics reminiscent of Byzantium an immense collection particularly rich in Greek manuscripts and printed books. Séguier favored Greek works in order to foster Father Joseph's policy of rapprochement between Eastern Christians and the Roman Church.[1]

It is not surprising, therefore, that specialized booksellers and people acting as procurers tried to obtain from ancient Oriental and Occidental libraries manuscripts that were valuable for either their illuminations or their texts. It is also to be expected that princes and ministers went to any length to acquire such rare objects. However, in addition, this mode of collecting became a firmly established behavior pattern among all the elite classes in France. Each individual was bent on acquiring a library equal to his status. In my thesis, I tried to demonstrate this point by devoting several chapters to analyzing the contents of libraries enumerated in the "inventories prepared after death" made for residents of Paris during the years 1600–1670. For at least two generations, the great magisterial and noble families had been establishing collections that by 1650 often contained several thousand large volumes sumptuously decorated with the arms of their owners. These libraries constituted an affirmation of their social rank. This passion for libraries is not surprising if one remembers, for example, that the collections of the presidents of sovereign courts served as documentation centers for the members of their entourage. In a similar fashion, doctors and lawyers often possessed libraries surpassing a thousand volumes, while the conseillers of sovereign courts and lesser persons, when they were not wealthy, had to be content with a few hundred volumes, or even with as little as fewer than a hundred. This passion for books was an attitude that newcomers tried to imitate, each in his own manner. For example, financiers, preferring form over substance, opted for books with illustrations.[2]

In general, the surviving inventories after death reveal a persistence of a conceptual framework based on respect for tradition. This framework can be detected in the accumulation of sacred texts, patristic texts, large compilations of Roman and canon law, and classical texts as well as historical treatises proclaiming the antiquity and grandeur of France and its kings. The collections enumerated reveal a somewhat rigid erudite humanism dominated by an interest, on the one hand, in Augustine, who appears to have enjoyed immense prestige after the beginning of the seventeenth century, and, on the other hand, in the ancient Stoics, in particular Seneca, whose philosophy was sometimes considered a pagan precursor of Christianity. However, when we take note of divergences from this somewhat conventional and balanced model, the inventories reveal instances of ultramontane or Gallican tendencies and occasionally even a certain skepticism and libertine mentality, especially among doctors. Finally, a few inventoried collections reflect more modern tastes. For example, certain maîtres des comptes and quite a few members of the world of letters were on occasion interested in the exact sciences.

However, the taste for erudition characteristic of these collections was not present in the aristocratic libraries. These reflected infinitely more worldly interests and a preference for books with illustrations. Moreover, the new spiritual literature seemed rarely to be found alongside the books of devotions, which were especially appreciated at the beginning of the century by the wives of great nobles as well as by a certain portion of the nobility of the robe. Finally, it is striking to note the rarity and poverty of the libraries of the merchants and bourgeois who seem at best to have been content with passing on from generation to generation a few volumes consisting of either the Bible, lives of the saints, or Plutarch's *Lives*.

Over the last ten years, there has been much criticism, and rightly so, of the usefulness of these library inventories as sources. For example, it has been noted frequently that the inventories did not record data that might indicate wear due to frequent use. It has also been remarked that the monuments of theology, gathered together in ecclesiastical establishments during the Counter-Reformation and surviving today in the public collections of France, show little evidence of wear and therefore appear to have been only rarely consulted. At the same time, the question has also been raised as to what degree the books assembled together in many large collections were ever read, since it is evident that many of the collections were purposely created simply by gathering large editions of out-of-date texts. One might also ask if the assembling of these costly monuments actually amounted to a proclamation of symbolic dependence on a culture that was already dead or at least moribund. In addition, it should not be forgotten that the list of books of someone who died in 1670 reflected the preoccupations of a man belonging to a generation that had been active between 1630 and 1640. Finally, the compilers of these inventories naturally tended to favor expensive books, that is, large reference works collected over generations, to the detriment of recent smaller books that were the messengers of the latest literary or intellectual currents. How can we otherwise explain that, judging from the inventories dating from the years prior to 1670, French literature seems to come to a halt with the generation of Montaigne, Bodin, and Charron? How is it to be imagined that the important spiritual authors, whose writings were published so often since the beginning of the seventeenth century, are not mentioned sooner or more often?

A SERIES OF RATHER EXCEPTIONAL DOCUMENTS will help us to fill the lacunae that I have just indicated. It consists of the account books of Jean II Nicolas, a bookseller from Grenoble, who left us a daily journal of the works that he purchased and sold from 1645 to 1668.[3]

First, let us examine the man. Jean II Nicolas was one of the descendants of a line of peddlers who had left their village or their mountainside to try to make their fortune. He and his ancestors, peddlers since the sixteenth century, came from the Oisans valley, a mountainous region south of Grenoble. They formed part of a mercantile network composed of men who issued from the same group of villages. This network stretched from northern Italy to Switzerland, to southern France, and of course to Paris.[4] They constituted a group of families united by bonds of kinship, each one of which had its own particular specialty. Viewed in a larger context, these families served to exploit both the manpower and capital resources of the mountains. The network to which the Nicolas family belonged proved to be particularly useful in a period when all long-distance exchange had to be based on shared trust.

Nicholas opened a shop in the quarter of the Palais de Justice in Grenoble. At that time, Grenoble was a city of 15,000 to 20,000 inhabitants. As capital of Dauphiné, it possessed numerous clergymen, a parlement, chambre des comptes, and a variety of lesser gentlemen of the robe and, of course, artisans and energetic merchants. Finally, the city housed a large Protestant minority to which our man Nicolas belonged. Here Nicolas combined the sale of books with that of medicine, spices, and paper goods. However, the core of his trade was to sell books and occasionally to publish them.

A large portion of the books that Jean Nicolas offered for sale were in Latin. These often included the works of Spanish or Italian jurists and theologians. However, it is striking that a great majority of books sold by Nicolas were in the French language. Earlier than sources would indicate for other regions, the residents of the Dauphiné learned to read the ancient classics as well as the Church fathers in their own language. Even more, they came to the store of our bookseller to gobble up the latest arrivals in French. For details on Nicolas's activities, I refer you to my two previous volumes on this subject. Suffice it here to say that even though he was a Protestant, Nicolas engaged in the active sale of Catholic books such as Richelieu's *Principaux points de la foi de l'Église catholique* as well as innumerable books of hours, the *De imitatione Christi,* and all sorts of spiritual and devotional texts, not to mention books of Catholic tracts against Protestants, anti-Capucin and anti-Jesuit pamphlets, and books of Jansenist propaganda, in particular, Pascal's *Lettres provinciales.* I shall pass over the texts of jurisprudence that were obligatorily present in legal circles. However, I must mention that Nicolas, who even sold children's schoolbags, did a brisk business in schoolbooks, usually those composed by the Jesuits. Moreover, the Grenoblois purchased important quantities of legal orations and collections of sermons in French. With true passion, they followed the efforts of Godeau, Desmaretz de Saint-Sorlin, Le Moyne, the de Scudérys, and Chapelain to endow French letters with Christian and national epics.

I must stress that the principal interests of Nicolas's clients were primarily concentrated on two sectors. The first of these concerned literature that was entirely contemporary. As the result of some felicitous discoveries, it has long been known that Grenoble was distinguished by the movement toward literary affectation or preciousness. Particularly in the summer, magistrates and gentlemen of the robe migrated to their properties in Bas-Dauphiné around the Côte-Saint-André, where they received each other and exchanged poems and epigrams. Far from Paris, Parisian manners were adopted much more quickly than might have been thought. Thus, Voiture was especially appreciated in the salons of Dauphiné where one sought the novels of Alemán, Quevedo, or Cervantes, as well as those of Sorel,

Gomberville, La Calprenède, and, in particular, those of Mlle. de Scudéry. Nicolas sold her works for the astronomical price of twelve livres per volume, or he would rent them for six livres. Similarly, the arrival of traveling theatrical troops, notably that of Molière in 1654 and 1658, attracted the high society of the city to an indoor tennis court for an evening of entertainment. It is not surprising, therefore, that Nicolas agreed to accept on consignment thirty-six copies of the *Traité héraldique du Languedoc* by Joseph Béjart, Molière's brother-in-law, and that he regularly sold the plays of Boyer, Boisrobert, Guérin de Bouscal, La Serre, Le Royer, Mareschal, Du Ryer, Rotrou, and Scarron. Nor can we be astonished that he sold Corneille's plays in counterfeit editions that were printed in Avignon by the dozens and at low prices (such as *Polyeucte, Héraclius,* and *Andromède*).

Finally, the milieux of Grenoble seemed to have a passion for history, especially recent history. The propaganda orchestrated by royal historiographers was loudly echoed. In particular, the magistrates of Dauphiné were very fond of current events. This explains the success here of the Lyon reprints of the *Gazette,* subscriptions to which were sold for twelve livres a year. Nicolas also lent the *Gazette* for half the price at a clip of fifty copies a week. It is understandable that under these conditions certain Mazarinades, that is, those concerning the Fronde in Bordeaux and especially the imprisonment of princes, were widely diffused in the same milieu. It is equally understandable that in such a troubled climate, the execution of Charles I of England had great impact on men's minds, perhaps even acting as an antidote to rebellion. Nicolas reprinted a narrative of this event in a thousand copies.

Nicolas's business accounts similarly give us a better idea of what the reading public of Grenoble was like. While the merchants and artisans returned often to Nicolas's shop to purchase feather pens or blocks of paper, they rarely bought books except when, as recently elected consuls, they became part of the parish gentry and felt the need to constitute a library appropriate to their new rank. Slightly better clients, the notaires, procurers, and captaines-châtelaines of the provostship, sometimes came to his store to buy a few schoolbooks for their children, a book of hours for their wives, and, on occasion, editions of plays. Some lawyers did not have the means to do much better, and as a result, in the end, purchasers of books in Grenoble were recruited mainly among the most successful lawyers and especially the magistrates. The most frequent buyers were the members of the parlement, the maîtres des comptes, and most notably, the presidents of the courts who belonged to a select group of families that set the tone for the rest of the upper crust of the city.

Among these influential readers could be found Hector d'Agoult, scion of an old provincial family, who married Uranie de Calizon, daughter of one of the great figures of the period, the chancellor of Navarre and confidant of Henri IV. Uranie's aunt Lucrèce married a conseiller in the parlement. How could one not be precious in one's tastes or deeply interested in Parisian literature with such affinities? Other influential readers included the husbands of two daughters of Guichard Déagent, the rich financier and natural father of the famous Parisian bookseller Barbou. One of his daughters married Étienne Roux, a rich conseiller in the parlement; the other married the all-powerful Salvaing de Boissière, first president of the chambre des comptes and the intellectual wonder of Grenoble. Finally, there was François du Faure, Sieur de la Rivière, who had a brilliant career, ending up as a conseiller d'état and intendant of Languedoc. He was the father-in-law of Nicolas Prunier de Saint-André, conseiller in the parlement since 1635, who in 1655 became *president à mortier* of the parlement of Dauphiné and Marquis of Virieu. These people formed part of a society of closely related, highly cultivated people among whom it was considered good form to be an important purchaser of books.

While the possession of a library in Grenoble was clearly a sign of belonging to a particular social class, the daily purchases of Nicolas's clients reflected their veritable passion for reading as well as their very different personalities and opposing points of view. For example, there was the conseiller Roux, a tortured soul, who had been somewhat of a libertine in his youth when he had churned out many uncharitable satirical works to the great amusement of Dauphinois society. Shortly thereafter, we find him presiding over the *Compagnie du Très Saint Sacrement* of the city, buying pedagogical books for his sons who had a Jesuit tutor, or procuring simple pious books and catechisms in such large numbers that one wonders if he gave them away to those around him. All this did not prevent him from seeking to purchase those *florilegia* and compilations that were the precursors of our modern dictionaries, from being interested, for example, in the quarrels over chronology, and in particular, from purchasing the *Curiositez inouyes* of Gaffarel, the *Adagia* of Erasmus, the *De la sagesse* of Charron, the *Lettres* of Balzac, the *Socrates* of Heinsius, and the complete works of La Mothe Le Vayer—in short a literary corpus that could be described as certainly less than orthodox.

Thus, in the heart of Grenoble's varied milieu, changeable Monsieur Roux seemed to have been questioning himself. Could he even have been spying a little in the same city where another figure, the Abbot of Saint-Fermin, also a libertine from a very good family, was pondering over his *Aloysia Sigea,* a masterpiece of anti-Tridentine pornography that Nicolas's son would translate into French? However, not everyone displayed such an open mind. Alongside the sometimes troubled but nonetheless intellectually inquisitive mind of Étienne Roux, there was Monsieur Du Virrer, first vice-baili of Grésivaudan and then president of the chambre des comptes of Grenoble. Erudite that he was, he was impassioned for Roman and ecclesiastical history, and especially for the history of France. A jurist, he was interested enough in questions of sorcery to acquire Jean Bodin's *Démonomanie.* He was as adept as Roux within the republic of letters but in a different way. He acquired the epicurean studies of Gassendi, Gilles Ménage's *Origines de la langue française,* and Vaugelas's *Rémarques sur la langue française.* In contrast, he was indifferent toward contemporary French literature. One can readily imagine him in the act of reading some weighty treatise, while not far away Molière was presenting one of his plays.

Overall, when surveying the purchases of all these individuals, it is striking to note the degree of community of interest that united these Dauphinois families among whom there were so many mixed marriages. These, however, did not occur without provoking some conflict. There is the example of Alexandre de Bardonnenche, issued from the high nobility of Grenoble and a companion of the Constable of Lesdiguière during the wars. A Protestant, he married a Catholic woman. Two of his daughters were taken away from him and entered, or forced to enter, the religious life. A faithful royalist who subscribed to the *Gazette,* this eminently respectable man on occasion bought Calvinist booklets. However, he also procured Catholic books that were destined for his daughter Jeanne, to whom he promised in his will an important sum of money if she would repent and return to his faith. During this time, his son, Alexandre II, conseiller of the Protestant chambre de l'édit of the parlement of Dauphiné, divided his purchases between the most recent literature and books of Protestant piety. His wife, a great admirer of Corneille, figured among the leading devotees of literary preciousness in the city. However, this did not prevent her from refusing to recant her Protestant faith in 1685 and being "placed in a religious order," whereas her husband simply submitted to Catholicism.

The picture outlined thus far reveals an astonishing modernism and diversity among the Dauphinois. Perhaps as a consequence of the cohabitation of two religions, one remarks among certain Catholics of the region a form of anticlericalism that resembles that of the Calvinists. In particular, one notes the birth of a critical spirit that was spawned by the controversies surrounding the Mass and the Virgin Mary. There was present, dare I say the word, a certain skepticism.

Was it just another consequence of this situation that the Grenoblois appeared singularly open to new philosophical and scientific books, especially those coming from England and Holland? These books were so popular that Cureau de la Chambre's *Traité des passions de l'âme* was the object of a local counterfeit edition as was Joseph Hall's *Considérations fortuites*. Equally appreciated were the *The Life of Epicurus* and other diverse publications of Gassendi, who was almost a neighbor, and the works of Bacon and Grotius. In particular, a small group of Grenoblois sought after and read Descartes's *Discours de la méthode* and his other works, Harvey's *De Moto cordis*, Blaise Pasacal's *Traité de l'équilibre des liqueurs,* and Father Mersenne's *Observationes physicomathematicae,* not to mention the diverse writings of Hobbes and Milton. These difficult works undoubtedly passed from hand to hand and were openly debated in the salons of Grenoble. In this milieu one can observe an intellectual evolution that Parisian inventories reflect only at the end of the century.

THE REVOCATION OF THE EDICT OF NANTES must have had a particular impact on a mixed urban population like that of Grenoble. One has only to scan the police reports concerning the attitudes of the "newly converted" in the years following 1685 to understand the noxious atmosphere in which the elite of Grenoble were obliged to live. It quickly becomes more understandable why there developed in this city a climate of opposition to absolutism and the ideologies supporting it. The edict's revocation also resulted in the flight from France of the Protestant elites, including many Calvinist printers and publishers, many of whom fled to the dynamic Low Countries, but also to Berlin, London, and Geneva, completely upsetting the publishing landscape of Europe.

In the previous chapters we have seen that at the beginning of the seventeenth century the Dutch book industry underwent a rapid expansion, which undoubtedly was related to the development of an internal market. However, the publishers of

Holland, like those of Antwerp earlier, were also by vocation exporters whose biggest problem was finding texts to print. The Roman Index provided them with an excellent catalog of "best sellers" that they were quick to promote systematically. Because of its vocation as a commercial intermediary between Germanic Europe and the francophone regions, Holland found it natural to assume the diffusion of French books in the east at a time when German princely courts were beginning to take a great interest in French literature. As a result, the Dutch successfully inundated the German market with French titles, as has been documented in an excellent inquiry on the provenance of French works in the ducal library of Wolfenbüttel.[5] They produced editions of such high quality that they were in great demand even in France. But this did not satisfy the voracious appetite of Dutch presses. They undertook to print and diffuse everything that had been prohibited in France. The Jansenists who took refuge in the Austrian Low Countries, where they maintained excellent relations with the Elzevirs and their emulators, acted in the same manner. This situation became infinitely more serious when after the revocation of the Edict of Nantes, the Low Countries welcomed refugees such as Bayle, Jurieu, or La Roque, to name only the principal figures. From then on, the gazettes printed in Holland played an essential role in intellectual developments. At Rotterdam, Reinier Leers developed a printing establishment that built its fortune on Bayle's famous dictionary.[6]

In conclusion, this state of affairs calls for two final thoughts. First, a historian of the book cannot help but be struck by the technical quality of the Dutch editions of this period that were always produced with the greatest care. Second, absolutism paid the price for the choice it had made at the time of Richelieu to favor the *écrivains* who, because they sought to flatter the king and his ministers, were more malleable than the members of the *Respublica litteraria*. For the intellectuals who opposed Louis XIV during the second part of his reign were at once the descendants of the members of the *Respublica litteraria* and the precursors of the men of the Enlightenment. Thus, in the final analysis, Dutch and to a lesser degree Swiss publishers were assured of an indisputable ascendancy over their Parisian counterparts who, protected by excessive privilèges, had totally lost their capacity for innovation.

INTELLECTUAL ABSOLUTISM, which had known its brief period of glory at the beginning of the reign of Louis XIV, could henceforth only engender a growing perversion attested to by the history of Rouennais printing, a subject that has recently been brilliantly delineated by Jean-Dominique Mellot.[7] Rouen was the third most important printing center of France since the sixteenth century and the capital of a rich province. With easy access to the Low Countries, to London and England, and finally farther away to Spain, it was the outer port of Paris. Beginning in the seventeenth century, the number of printers and booksellers grew without cease, with printing shops increasing from twenty-eight to fifty-four between 1610 and 1660. At the same time, people of the book trades spread out across the city. The principal publishers and booksellers continued to locate themselves in the courtyard of the Palais where they found a rich and numerous clientele. Others grouped themselves around the cathedral in front of the *portail des libraires,* as had been traditional since medieval times. However, among the newcomers, some congregated around the very important Jesuit college, and others, who were already specializing in the publishing and sale of so-called "popular" books, settled in the quarter of Saint-Jean. Finally, the Protestant minority possessed their own bookstores located close to their temple.

Rich and literate for the period, the city of Rouen offered important possibilities that might have tended to favor the development of a subsistence economy. However, the Normans were an energetic people and succeeded in continuously enlarging the field of their activities by frequently changing their orientation. The secret of their success can be found in the numerous examples of solidarity that existed in this particularly homogeneous collectivity. Rouennais printing shops were singularly modest, but they had the capacity to perform remarkably due to their internal organization. According to general custom, not a single journeyman could be hired from outside the city. The same was true, or nearly so, for apprentices beginning in 1615 when the printing families then established in Rouen began to refuse to hire all newcomers. Instead, the heads of shops found their labor force in their own households where their children qualified as "masters" early on, but for a long time remained as "maîtres à gage," hired masters who worked like journeymen either for their parents or their colleagues. The closed character of this society for a long time led it to refuse the monarchy's request to hand over a list of its workers. Among the heads of shops, solidarity was the rule, and it was practiced in a fashion strangely reminiscent of that of the Stationer's Company of London. Thus for the benefit of the community they agreed to form groups, often including up to twenty or forty shops, to publish specific works of which the sales were assured. Such joint ventures included Pajot's Latin dictionary and Senault's *Usage des passions* published in astronomically large editions of 5,000 to 10,000 copies. It is mind-boggling to imagine the complexity of the relations that Rouennais printers had to maintain in order to organize such mass production.

In addition, the parlement of Rouen, although it had agreed to record the Edict of Moulins in order to support the king against the papacy, continued nevertheless to distribute privilèges to those residing under its jurisdiction to print locally. This practice seems to have been maintained with the tacit approval of the monarchy. In addition, the parlement encouraged the city's booksellers and printers to develop for the books falling in the public domain a copyright system whereby everyone had the right to register the title of the work he was planning to publish in order to conserve an exclusive right to it.

One might well imagine that these corporatist attitudes would engender a kind of turning inwards, but this was not at all the case. The expansionist policies of the Rouennais printers were singularly encouraged during the first two-thirds of the seventeenth century by the role that some of their compatriots played in the literary world. This activity assured Rouennais editions a national status. Thus at the beginning of the century a Rouennais printer, Raphael Du Petit Val, numbered among the great literary publishers of his time, published some of the collections of poetry that were the precursors of our literary revues.[8] The printers of Rouen offered prices that defied all competition for a product that was generally correct, and thereby they literally undertook the conquest of the Parisian publishing business. In this, they had the assistance of Corneille who, wishing to supervise personally the printing of his own works, entrusted their production beginning in 1642 to the Rouennais printer Laurent Maurry. Finally, profiting from their geographic location, they undertook increasingly regular contacts, first with the southern Low Countries and subsequently with the northern Low Countries, where they benefited from the favorable attitudes shown toward their colleagues who belonged to the so-called Reformed Church, men such as Lucas, Cailloué, and Berthelin.

For a long time, the Rouennais succeeded in remaining prosperous in this way. However, beginning in the 1660s, their activities began to show signs of running out of steam. From then on, the Parisian booksellers, assured of the monarchy's support, were able to monopolize the grants of royal licenses, and more significantly, the prolongation of existing privilèges, thereby opening a breach in the Rouennais system of receiving local privilèges for publication. This precipitated a series of judicial cases before courts in Paris that the Rouennais consistently lost in spite of the support of their parlement. Consequently, many printers fell back on local publications, and municipal commissions. Here, as elsewhere, the book professions began to suffer from the problem of overproduction, and members of printing families began to leave the city to seek their fortune elsewhere, swarming in particular to other Norman cities that were eager to establish their own printing shops. So severe were the problems, that the usual need to find someone to blame led Catholic publishers to view unfavorably their Protestant colleagues who constituted a dynamic and closed minority. Catholic booksellers were, therefore, not greatly upset by the revocation of the Edict of Nantes, which broke up the Protestant group and encouraged the most enterprising among them to seek their fortune elsewhere. In some cases these émigrés founded flourishing establishments in Holland by using their former business connections to inundate France with their production.

Is it necessary to add that these expulsions did not settle the economic problems? The remaining Rouennais printers and booksellers had to reorient their own activities and create for themselves new opportunities right in their own province. Throughout the century, urban popular education had developed, and the countryside of upper Normandy acquired numerous parish schools. It was not surprising therefore that the two principal printing shops of the city, those of the widow Oursel and Jean-Baptist Lallemand, devoted themselves at the beginning of the eighteenth century to printing books adapted to this new public. The works they published included ancient chivalric romances, books of piety, or simple moral texts, and short treatises on cooking, gardening, and agriculture, and other titles beginning *Secrétaire à la mode* . . . . This kind of specialization had developed only gradually, but its importance became apparent only during this period, and certain of its unorthodox aspects did not take long to pose problems.

These new markets were insufficient, however. Faced with the Parisian cornering of titles, the Rouennais made counterfeiting books a sort of municipal sport. Moreover, they did not lack the means to give the Parisians a good fight for their money. In point of fact, how could a bundle thrown out onto the banks of the Seine from a passing barge be intercepted? How could the author and publisher of an illicit book be identified when the whole city was in cahoots?

The following two cases demonstrate that in these situations the efforts of the police were always foiled. The great Arnauld, exiled for his Jansenist beliefs, avidly attended to the distribution of the pamphlets that he hoped to see circulated throughout France. Needless to say, he had the assistance of other fanatics. On 9 October 1682, at the Hôtel-Dieu of Saint-Denis, the police seized some bundles of Jansenist books and arrested a certain Dubois, chaplain of the establishment, and a priest from Rouen named Jean Racine, who was in possession of documents signed by one Urbain Deville. After an investigation, it became apparent that the head of the network, this pseudonymous Deville, was none other than the priest of Saint-Ouen of Rouen, an Oratorian, Father Du Breuil. Du Breuil was a prominent personality in the city. It was also learned that he had acted in connection with a certain Perroté, the secretary of the intendant Le Blanc, who was a protégé of Colbert. The minister immediately notified Le Blanc, but he was unable to discover anything. It became clear that Perroté, who was in fact the second husband of Le Blanc's mother, had acted in close conjunction with the intendant and that the latter had falsified with his own hand a customs document in order to allow Arnauld's shipments to enter France.

Each day opposition gained more ground. Hoping to put some order in the affairs of Rouen, the monarchy made the mistake of permitting a certain Boisguilbert, well known for his heretical views, to be named lieutenant général de police. Empowered to authorize the printing of local works of less than two pages, it was not long before he used his prerogative in a somewhat special manner to protect the local commerce. The moment arrived when the Paris police lieutenant, the famous d'Argenson, stopped the publication of a work entitled *L'état présent des affaires de France* that was identified as being a Rouennais printing, authored by a private individual of the city. The intendant was alerted, but he learned nothing more after questioning all the concerned Rouennais. Moreover, the authorities failed to interrogate the lieutenant de police, Boisguilbert, whose opinions were only too well known and who, it later became apparent, was the author of the work in question. Such a situation obviously demanded correction. Abbot Bignon was put in charge of the proceedings. No one was more suited to this task than this brilliant and powerful nobleman, a nephew of Chancellor Pontchartrain, who was connected to Fontenelle. Bignon, because of his fidelity to his concubine with whom he had a daughter, was blocked from becoming a bishop. Nevertheless, he played a long and essential role in the evolution of French letters. Named directeur de la librairie, Bignon began an important investigation. He took a census of all the printing shops and bookstores in each French city and arbitrarily limited their number, as had already been done for Paris. Most significantly, he extended the system of privilèges by declaring that no work, old or new, could be published without first obtaining a general or local privilège or a permission bearing the great seal of the royal chancellery.

It remained to be seen whether the provincial printing industry would be brought to a state of quasi ruin by the new obligation to engage at every juncture in costly proceedings in Paris and by strict application of asphyxiating new regulations. This question was starkly posed on two occasions at the end of the reign of Louis XIV. Forced to submit the titles of the popular booklets that they published, Rouennais booksellers indicated that these works were destined for the education of country people and were sold by the dozen to the country merchants. They then sent them in large numbers, in the hope that they would not be read, to be stamped with the royal seal. Provincial publishers still could not prevent supercilious censors from refusing to print works published since time immemorial but now judged to be "impertinent" or exhibiting "excessive liberties." Gradually, however, Paris authorities became aware of the economic strength of this new popular market, and finally under the continued pressure of the market and booksellers, Bignon reckoned that "the best way of inhibiting abuses was to provide the book trades with a reasonable degree of liberty." He therefore decided to grant an exception for this genre of book by conferring on them a general permission to publish while at the same time purging 28 percent of the titles from the permitted list. Thus, the new imposition of controls in 1709 was accompanied by sufficient flexibility to permit publishers to carry out their business without always having to obtain authorization from the Parisian authorities.

Significantly, these same booksellers, supported by their parlement, had begun to request systematically licenses for printing books of dubious nature published abroad. Naturally, these requests were refused. However, the office of the directeur de la librairie realized that it had refused because of questions of principle the printing of works within France that were being distributed there anyway by foreign presses. Under these conditions, the same Abbot Bignon in agreement with the intendants gave tacit permission to print works of this type, which Bignon enumerated in nothing but a letter (1709).[9] Thus was born the strangest system of censorship ever created by the ancien régime, for soon, the office of the directeur de la librairie, always preoccupied with details and procedures, wished to create a formal register of these tacit permissions (1718). However, it was forced shortly thereafter to institute a decentralizing measure when it made the first president of the parlement of Normandy the directeur de la librairie of his province, empowering him to grant the authorizations in question on the spot. Thus was revealed the irrationality of a system that was both too Cartesian and too Catholic, and that in the end generated its own casuistry.

THE ABSOLUTISM THAT HAD BECOME A DOCTRINE in France after the Wars of Religion and that reached its apogee during the first part of the personal reign of Louis XIV finally foundered in the midst of its own contradictions. The Very Christian King, having become the King of Glory and of national heroes and being persuaded that he was as infallible as the pope, had wished to think in place of his subjects. However, the bureaucratic logic that issued from such a system found itself, as in all antiquated French governments, increasingly unable to adapt to reality. During this time, England, which had killed its king, was also undergoing a difficult education in freedom of the press and parliamentary government. Can one not think that from then on the die was cast and the Revolution of 1789 was already on the horizon?

Fig. 4. Thucydides, *Histoire de la guerre du Péloponèse*, 1527

Fig. 5. A translation of Diodorus Siculus by Antoine Macault, being read aloud to Francis I

Varii, iidémque noui

literarum, & notarum characteres, quibus no-
bis ad perfectiorem vocum Gallicarum repræ-
sentationem vtendum fuit, quorú rationes suis
locis redduntur.

i- u-, pro i u consonantibus,vt i-a, u-ái:id est,iam,vado.
é, sonum habens plenum,vt charitas charité,amatus amé.
è, sonum habens exilem,vt gratia gracé,bona bonè.
ē, sonum habens medium,vt amate áimes.
ü,u per o pronútiatum Latinis ,ante m & n propè semper:
   cuius loco Galli o ferè supponunt.
ç, c sono s,vt Alençon,id est Alenconium vrbs.
ç̃, c sono duorum ss,vt pôíçer,id est picare.
c̃, c sono ch,vt cêu-al,id est caballus.
g̃, g sono prope gua,gue,gui,guo,guu.vt g̃allè, id est cal-
   lus vel galla. Volg̃e,id est vulgus & vulgi tauor.g̃ilbert &
   Gilbert,id est Gilbertus.g̃org̃e,id est guttur,a gurges.
g-,g sono ferè i-a,i-è,i-i,i-o,i-u.vt g-ambè,à g-amba,
   g-è,id est ego.g-ilbert,a Gilbertus,g-óie,id est gaudium.
ǧ, g sono s,vt lǧons,id est legamus.
î, í sono obscuro, vt mâîstrè,id est magister.
s̃, s truncato sibilo in fine dictionis.sic etiam
t̃, t̃, & cæteræ similiter consonantes, vt les̃ bones̃ bêstes̃.
áí,éí,óí,óý,áü,éü,óü,diphthongorú notæ,vt máí,pléín,
   móí,moý,cáúse, flêúr,póúr,id est maius, plenus, mihi,
   mei,caúsa,flos,pro.
áí,éí,óí,óý,áü,éü,óü,vocalium earundem diuisarú notæ.
êü, êü sed sono dilutiore & exiliore , vt êcúr,mêúrt, id est
   cor,moritur.

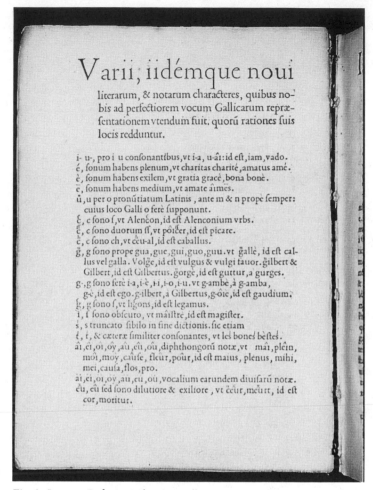

Fig. 6. Jacques Dubois, *In linguam gallicum isagoge,* 1532

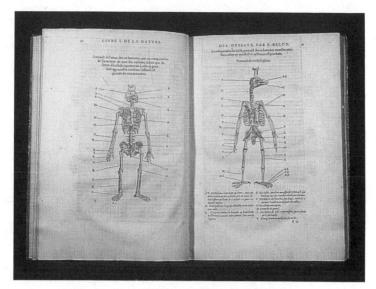

Fig. 7. Jean Belon, *Histoire de la nature des oiseaux*, 1555

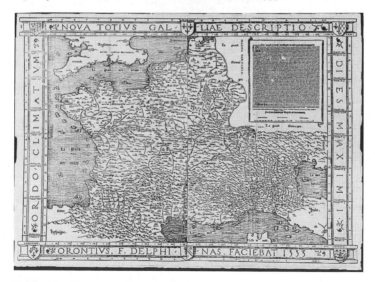

Fig. 8. The first map of France, by Oronce Fine, 1475

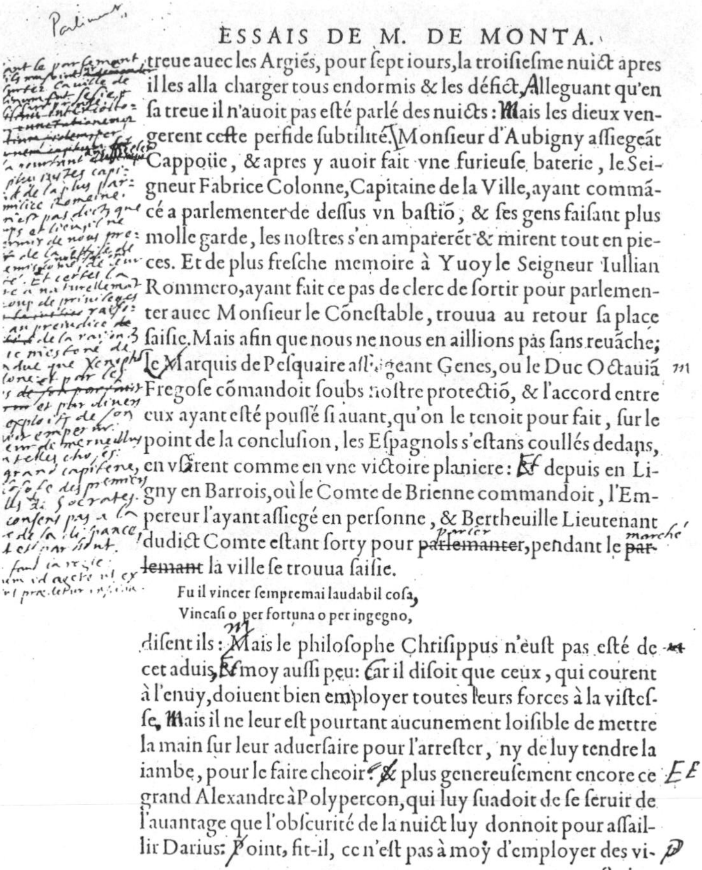

treue auec les Argiés, pour sept iours, la troisiesme nuict apres
il les alla charger tous endormis & les défict. Alleguant qu'en
sa treue il n'auoit pas esté parlé des nuicts : Mais les dieux ven-
gerent ceste perfide subtilité. Monsieur d'Aubigny assiegeát
Cappoüe, & apres y auoir fait vne furieuse baterie , le Seigneur Fabrice Colonne, Capitaine de la Ville, ayant commá-
cé a parlementer de dessus vn bastió , & ses gens faisant plus
molle garde, les nostres s'en amparerét & mirent tout en pie-
ces. Et de plus fresche memoire à Yuoy le Seigneur Iullian
Rommero, ayant fait ce pas de clerc de sortir pour parlementer auec Monsieur le Conestable, trouua au retour sa place
saisie. Mais afin que nous ne nous en aillions pas sans reuáche;
le Marquis de Pesquaire assiegeant Genes, ou le Duc Octauiá
Fregose cómandoit soubs nostre protectió, & l'accord entre
eux ayant esté poussé si auant, qu'on le tenoit pour fait , sur le
point de la conclusion, les Espagnols s'estans coullés dedans,
en vsèrent comme en vne victoire planiere : Et depuis en Li-
gny en Barrois, où le Comte de Brienne commandoit , l'Em-
pereur l'ayant assiegé en personne, & Bertheuille Lieutenant
dudict Comte estant sorty pour ~~parlemanter~~, pendant le par-
~~lemant~~ la ville se trouua saisie.

Fu il vincer sempre mai laudabil cosa,
Vincasi o per fortuna o per ingegno,

disent ils : Mais le philosophe Chrisippus n'eust pas esté de
cet aduis, & moy aussi peu: Car il disoit que ceux , qui courent
à l'enuy, doiuent bien employer toutes leurs forces à la vistes-
se, Mais il ne leur est pourtant aucunement loisible de mettre
la main sur leur aduersaire pour l'arrester , ny de luy tendre la
iambe, pour le faire cheoir. & plus genereusement encore ce
grand Alexandre à Polypercon, qui luy suadoit de se seruir de
l'auantage que l'obscurité de la nuict luy donnoit pour assail-
lir Darius: Point, fit-il, ce n'est pas à moy d'employer des vi-
ctoires

Fig. 9. Montaigne, *Essais*

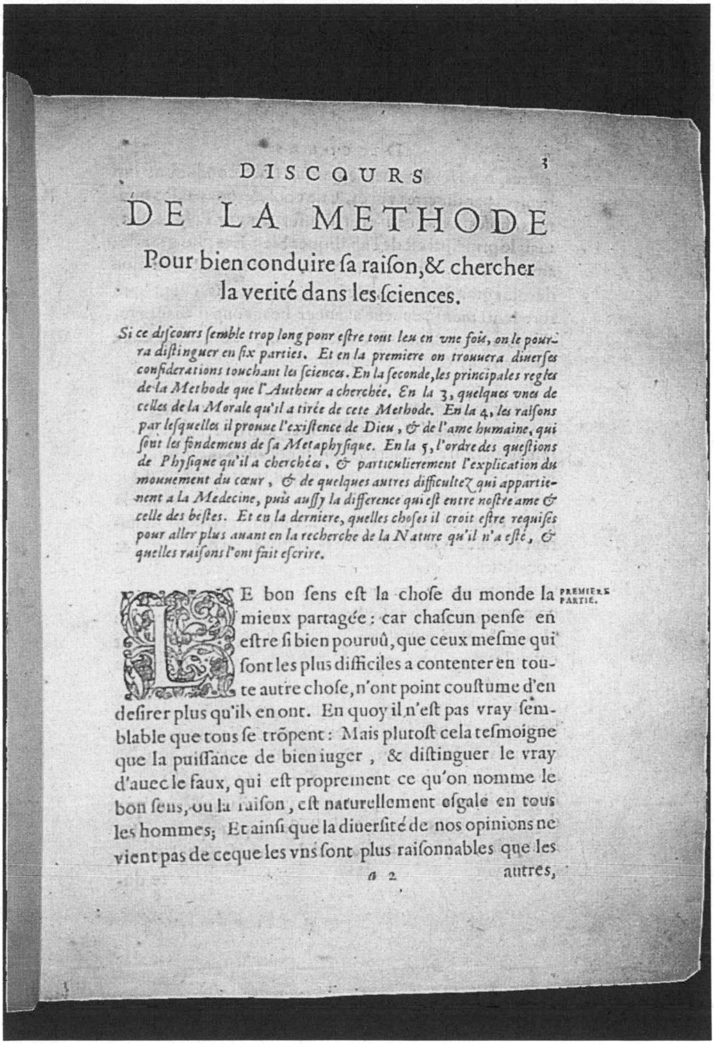

DE LA METHODE

Pour bien conduire ſa raiſon, & chercher la verité dans les ſciences.

Si ce diſcours ſemble trop long ponr eſtre tout leu en vne fois, on le pour-
ra diſtinguer en ſix parties. Et en la premiere on trouuera diuerſes
conſiderations touchant les ſciences. En la ſeconde, les principales regles
de la Methode que l'Autheur a cherchée. En la 3. quelques vnes de
celles de la Morale qu'il a tirée de cete Methode. En la 4. les raiſons
par leſquelles il prouue l'exiſtence de Dieu, & de l'ame humaine, qui
ſont les fondemens de ſa Metaphyſique. En la 5. l'ordre des queſtions
de Phyſique qu'il a cherchées, & particulierement l'explication du
mouuement du cœur, & de quelques autres difficultez qui appartie-
nent a la Medecine, puis auſſy la difference qui eſt entre noſtre ame &
celle des beſtes. Et en la derniere, quelles choſes il croit eſtre requiſes
pour aller plus auant en la recherche de la Nature qu'il n'a eſté, &
quelles raiſons l'ont fait eſcrire.

L E bon ſens eſt la choſe du monde la PREMIERE PARTIE.
mieux partagée : car chaſcun penſe en
eſtre ſi bien pouruû, que ceux meſme qui
ſont les plus difficiles a contenter en tou-
te autre choſe, n'ont point couſtume d'en
deſirer plus qu'ils en ont. En quoy il n'eſt pas vray ſem-
blable que tous ſe trôpent : Mais plutoſt cela teſmoigne
que la puiſſance de bien iuger , & diſtinguer le vray
d'auec le faux, qui eſt proprement ce qu'on nomme le
bon ſens, ou la raiſon, eſt naturellement eſgale en tous
les hommes; Et ainſi que la diuerſité de nos opinions ne
vient pas de ceque les vns ſont plus raiſonnables que les

autres,

Fig. 10. Descartes, *Discours de la méthode,* 1637

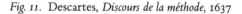

Fig. 11. Descartes, *Discours de la méthode,* 1637

Fig. 12. Pascal, *Essai pour les coniques*

Gloria immortalis labore parta.

*Ad reuerendiſſ.Cardinal.Granuella-
num Ant. Perrenotum.*

*Tortilis, & caudam ore tenens hic termite lauri
   Ambitur anguis, & ligonem circuit.
Gloria continuos nunquam moritura labores
   Sequitur, virens'que in ore viuit perpetim.*

                    A 5   Impu-

Fig. 13. Adrianus Junius, *Emblematum libellus,* 1565

V.

Memento, quæſo, quòd ſicut lutum feceris me, & in pulverem
reduces me. *Iob.* 10.

C Redideram Superis procul eſſe oblivia regnū,
  Resque ſuas memori Numina ferre ſinu:
Serpit at hîc Superis, video, quoq; metibus error,
  Aut aliquem ſimulant Numina cauta dolum.
Tu vel es, aut certè cupis immemor eſſe videri,
  Qui dubitas proprium quale creatis opus.
Si neſcis, referam; ſi ſcis, cur fingere pergis?
  Me Tua de luteâ dextera fecit humo.
Quæris ubi? toto locus eſt notiſſimus orbe,
  Primus ubi pater eſt conditus, hortus erat.
Fons ubi de riguis argenteus exilit herbis,
  Quadruplicíque ſuas flumine findit aquas.
Scire lubet tempus? minimo poſt tempore, ſalſa
  Cum maris aggeribus terra coëgit aquas.
Addo, (quod hiſtoriæ facit, hâc quoq; parte, pro-
  Puniceo rubuit Dædala gleba ſolo. [bandæ)
Hinc tritus et modicam digitis admenſus arenam,
  Primáque maſſa mei corporis illa fuit.
Nec primis erit his natalibus exitus impar,
  Nil niſi pulvis eram, nil niſi pulvis ero.
Sic faber argillam ſamiis dum repperit agris,
  Ædificat facili pocula ficta luto.

C 5 Principiò,

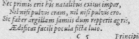

Memento, quæſo, quòd ſicut lutum feceris me,
& in pulverem reduces me. Iob. 10.

V.

Fig. 14. Hermann Hugo, S.J., *Pia desideria,* 1628

Fig. 15. *Imago primi saeculi Societatis Jesu*, 1640

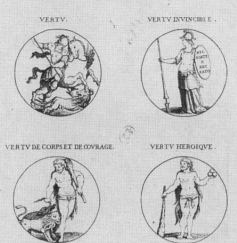

VERTV.   VERTV INVINCIBLE.

VERTV DE CORPS ET DE COVRAGE.   VERTV HEROIQVE.

✣✣✣✣✣✣✣✣✣✣✣✣✣✣✣✣

DIVERSES VERTVS.

A Vertu nous est representée en general, par vne belle & agreable Fille, qui a des aisles au dos, vne Picque en la main droite, en la gauche vne Couronne de Laurier, & vn Soleil resplendissant dans son beau sein.

Elle est peinte ieune, à cause qu'elle ne vieillit iamais, & que sa vigueur qui s'augmente de iour en iour, dure autant que la vie de l'homme.

Ses aisles demonstrent que la Vertu a cela de propre de s'esleuer par dessus le vol des personnes vulgaires, afin de iouïr de ces plaisirs perdurables, ausquels prennent part les seuls vertueux.

Le Soleil qu'on luy donne pour Symbole, nous fait connoi-

L ij

Fig. 16. Cesare Ripa, *Iconologia,* 1636

Fig. 17. Ronsard, *Oeuvres*, 1609

Fig. 18. Barberini, *Poemata,* 1634

Fig. 19. Louis de Blois, *Opera,* 1632

PVBLII
VIRGILII
MARONIS
OPERA

PARISIIS
E TYPOGRAPHIA REGIA ANNO MDCXLI

Fig. 20. Virgil, *Opera,* 1641

BIBLIA SACRA
PARISIIS MDCXLII
E TYPOGRAPHIA REGIA.

N. Poussin in.   Mellan f.

Fig. 21. Biblia sacra, 1642

Fig. 22. Blaise de Vigenère, *Les images ou tableaux de platte peinture des deux Philostrate,* 1614

Fig. 23. Blaise de Vigenère, *Les images ou tableaux de platte peinture des deux Philostrate*, 1614

Fig. 24. Corneille, *Horace*, 1641

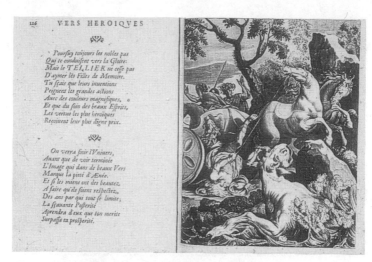

Pourſuy toûjours les nobles pas
Qui te conduiſent vers la Gloire:
Mais le TELLIER ne ceſſe pas
D'aymer les Filles de Memoire.
Tu ſçais que leurs inuentions
Peignent les grandes actions
Auec des couleurs magnifiques,
Et que du ſoin des beaux Eſprits,
Les vertus les plus heroïques
Reçoiuent leur plus digne prix.

On verra finir l'Vniuers,
Auant que de voir terminée
L'Image qui dans de beaux Vers
Marque la pieté d'Ænée.
Et ſi les miens ont des beautez,
A faire qu'ils ſoient reſpectez,
Des ans par qui tout ſe limite;
La ſçauante Poſterité
Aprendra d'eux que ton merite
Surpaſſa ta proſperité.

Fig. 25. Tristan l'Hermite, *Les vers héroïques*, 1648

Fig. 26. P. Le Moyne, S.J., *Les peintures morales*, 1641–43

Fig. 27. Desmarets de Saint-Sorlin, *Ariane*, 1639

Fig. 28. Desmarets de Saint-Sorlin, *Ariane*, 1639

Fig. 29. Georges de Scudéry, *Alaric ou Rome vaincue*, 1654

Fig. 30. Chapelain, *La pucelle ou la France délivrée,* 1656

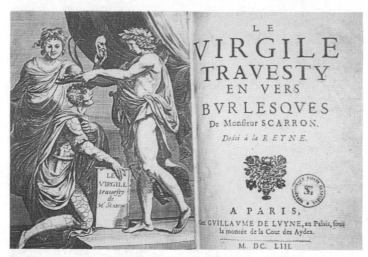

Fig. 31. Scarron, *Le Virgile travesty en vers burlesques*, 1648–51

Fig. 32. Thomas Billon, *Sibylla gallica*, 1624

Fig. 33. Valdor, *Les triomphes de Louis le Juste,* 1649

Fig. 34. Valdor, *Les triomphes de Louis le Juste,* 1649

Fig. 35. L'entrée triomphante de leurs Majestez Louis XIV . . . et Marie Thérèse d'Autriche . . . dans la ville de Paris, 1662

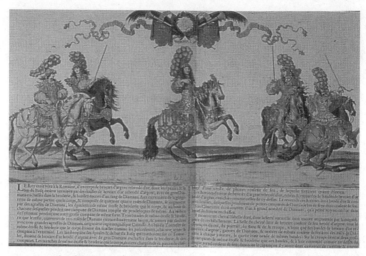

Fig. 36. Charles Perrault, *Les couses de tetes et de bagues faites par le Roy et par les Princes en l'année 1662,* 1670

Dans ces portraits on voit LOUIS également,
Il ne reste plus pour sa gloire,
Qu'à trouver vn autheur qui puisse dans l'histoire
Le peindre aussy fidelement. *Pavillon F. 1702*

Fig. 37   *Médailles des principaux événements du règne de Louis XIV,* 1702

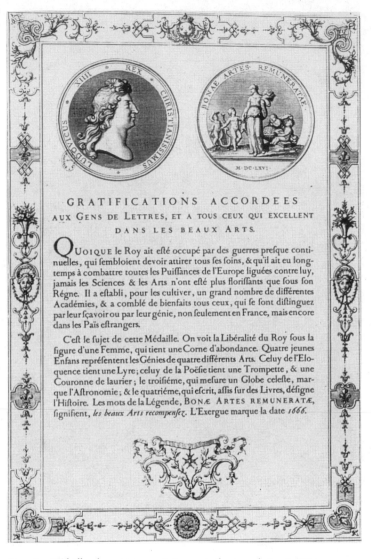

GRATIFICATIONS ACCORDEES
AUX GENS DE LETTRES, ET A TOUS CEUX QUI EXCELLENT
DANS LES BEAUX ARTS.

QUOIQUE le Roy ait esté occupé par des guerres presque conti-
nuelles, qui sembloient devoir attirer tous ses soins, & qu'il ait eu long-
temps à combattre toutes les Puissances de l'Europe liguées contre luy,
jamais les Sciences & les Arts n'ont esté plus florissants que sous son
Régne. Il a establi, pour les cultiver, un grand nombre de différentes
Académies, & a comblé de bienfaits tous ceux, qui se sont distinguez
par leur sçavoir ou par leur génie, non seulement en France, mais encore
dans les Païs estrangers.

C'est le sujet de cette Médaille. On voit la Libéralité du Roy sous la
figure d'une Femme, qui tient une Corne d'abondance. Quatre jeunes
Enfans représentent les Génies de quatre différents Arts. Celuy de l'Eloquence tient une Lyre; celuy de la Poësie tient une Trompette, & une
Couronne de laurier; le troisiéme, qui mesure un Globe celeste, marque l'Astronomie; & le quatriéme, qui escrit, assis sur des Livres, désigne
l'Histoire. Les mots de la Légende, BONÆ ARTES REMUNERATÆ,
signifient, *les beaux Arts recompensez*. L'Exergue marque la date *1666*.

Fig. 38. *Médailles des principaux événements du règne de Louis XIV,* 1702

CHAPTER 4

The French Classical Book: Text and Image

Historians must always remember that a text is by no means an abstract entity but rather a concrete object bearing many languages. Any serious study of the function that a book performs requires that one analyze the messages transmitted by the book while understanding how these messages are received. This is what I would like to do in this chapter for the French classical book while at the same time keeping open the possibility of going back to the early years of the sixteenth century when necessary.

It was, in fact, under François I that the modern French book began to take on its characteristic features. The adoption of Roman characters for the printing of books in the national language of France was then, as I have shown in chapter 2, the result of a concerted policy emanating from a specific group at the center of the royal entourage that included the clan of humanists grouped around Marguerite de Navarre, Guillaume Budé,

Clément Marot, and the secretaries of the king including Étienne Grolier, the illustrious bibliophile.

To give you an idea of what this veritable revolution was like, I will have to restrict myself to one book, the French translation of the *History of the Peloponnesian War* by the Greek historian Thucydides. This translation resulted from a royal request transmitted to bishop Claude de Seyssel during the reign of Louis XII, but the work did not appear until 1527. In the accompanying plate (fig. 4), you can see a copy of it, printed on vellum, that belonged to Louise de Savoie, the mother of François I and Margaret of Navarre.[1] You will note that in this copy there has been added in manuscript a ten-line stanza by the poet Clément Marot, who, it must be remembered, was Margaret's valet de chambre. This superb book, printed in 1,225 copies, was produced by the celebrated humanist printer Josse Bade for Jacques Colin, Secretaire de la Chambre du Roy and François I's personal reader.[2] It was followed by Diodorus Siculus's *History of the Successors of Alexander the Great,* translated into French by the same Seyssel.[3] A new translation of the same author[4] in 1535 contains an illustration that shows François I, surrounded by his courtiers, having the work read aloud (fig. 5). This clearly shows the importance that such publications assumed in the eyes of the sovereign.

I also explained in chapter 2 that the aim of this revolution in printing was not only to proclaim the equality of French to the classical languages but also to standardize it by establishing the speech of the Parisian court as the national language. Printing rendered French into a purer and more precise tongue in order ultimately to substitute it for Latin in legislative and judicial texts. This was the explanation of the initiatives taken by the celebrated printer Robert Estienne, who was very close to Guillaume Budé and Margaret of Navarre. Beginning in 1532 (1531 old style) and using type font attributed to the famous Garamond that was closely modeled on that of Aldus Manutius, Estienne published the first French grammar in France, composed by a Picard doctor named Jacques Dubois (in Latin, Sylvius), entitled *In linguam gallicam isagoge.*[5] At the beginning of the volume, Estienne included a table of signs, engraved in steel for the first time, in order to transcribe the sounds of the French language (fig. 6). These notably included the accents and auxiliary signs that are in use today such as the apostrophe, the diaeresis, and the circumflex, and his was the first attempt to distinguish the consonants i and u from the vowels i and u, the hard and soft g, and the hard and soft c. Subsequently, this same humanist printer (whom I personally consider to have been a genius) presented in a series of dictionaries the French translation of Latin words and expressions and published his own grammar.[6]

From then on, language became an instrument of royal policy, and such it remained. For the historian of the book this use of language can only be fully understood when viewed in the framework of a general evolution in the attitude of sixteenth-century men toward printed text and engravings. The middle of the sixteenth century was the period when people began to read maps and interpret images. The result was a prodigious outpouring of scientific illustrations dealing with anatomy, botany, zoology, and, indeed, even geography. This was a key phenomenon that I will confine myself to illustrating with two famous drawings. One is from Jean Belon's *Histoire de la nature des oiseaux* (1555)[7] in which the author stresses the homology of the human and bird skeleton (fig. 7). The other constitutes the first map of France (fig. 8) created by the illustrious Oronce Fine, the royal reader for mathematics.[8]

It is understandable under these conditions that French printers became concerned with making their texts less ambiguous. Thus, it was certainly not an accident that during this period the doctor Charles Estienne, Robert's brother, inspired by Italian models, published the first plays in the French language.[9] Most significantly, beginning with his initial editions, Estienne endeavored to provide at the very beginning of the play an explicit list of the characters, and he divided the acts into scenes, which until then had only been done in exceptional cases. Moreover, he preceded his publications with general introductions. This practice was continued by other printers who tried not only to present the dialogues clearly but also to give the reader a concrete notion of the staging and the setting where the action unfolded and of the elapse of time. This was an attempt to create a text format that singularly contrasts to that in vogue in Shakespeare's England. It also contributed, as I hope to demonstrate next, to conferring on French theater a set of rules for the textual presentation of plays that prefigured to a certain degree the famous classical rule of the three unities.

The modern book began to take on its own particular shape as can be seen by looking at Gabriello Simeoni's *Les illustres observations antiques* in the 1558 edition by the great Lyonnais printer Jean de Tournes. The page format appears to be completely modern as can be observed, for example, in the presentation of the title page and in the use of italic type for the preface and roman type for the text.

However, there is, to the modern eye, one surprising aspect of text presentation from this period. Very often, literary works in prose were printed continuously, that is, without paragraphs for pages on end. This characteristic is important when one considers that books today are laid out according to a plan by which the entire volume is divided into chapters and each chapter into a series of paragraphs, separated by blank spaces, permitting the eye to repose and the mind to assimilate better the elements contained in the preceding unity.

Certainly, a book designer like our printer Jean de Tournes was familiar with the chapter/paragraph form of presentation, for he employed it, among other instances, in a new edition of Comines's *Mémoires*. Therefore, it is all the more striking to observe that this mode of presentation remained infrequent for a long time among new French literary texts. Indeed, one notices a sort of hesitation, even a repugnance, on the part of French au-

thors to divide their vernacular texts in the modern fashion. For
example, the 1577 edition of Jean Bodin's *République* contained
only a very few paragraphs. However, in particularly deluxe editions such as André Thevet's *Singularités de la France antarctique,*
printed in Paris in 1558 by the heirs of Maurice de la Porte, side
notes printed in the margins offered a sort of schema parallel to
the text that performed a function similar to paragraphs.[10]

However, the most interesting case was clearly that of Montaigne. It is known that his *Essais* extend without any paragraphs sometimes for up to twenty-five pages (fig. 9). This form
of textual presentation can certainly be related to the stream of
reflection style characteristic of this celebrated author, but it in
no way means that this mode of presentation did not pose problems for him, witness the famous "Bordeaux copy," corrected
by his own hand in view of a new edition. In it, he tried to
give his text greater oratorical force by breaking it up. To this
end, he replaced commas and colons followed by minuscules at
the beginning of sentences and clauses with periods followed
by a capital. He explained his decision in the following manner:
"I want a language that has been cut up visually in which the
printer economizes neither periods nor capital letters. I myself
have often failed to remove commas and colons and have put
commas where there should have been periods." These remarks
clearly prove that Montaigne did not view the composition of
his texts as a modern author would and that Montaigne's conception ought to be taken into consideration by modern editors
who obstinately persist in arbitrarily breaking up his *Essais* into
paragraphs.[11]

In fact, the presentation of text in continuous blocks very
clearly corresponded to the concern that the prose writers of
this period had to imitate the traditional mode of presentation
of ancient Latin texts established by Aldus Manutius and his
imitators who did not separate the *capita* of their edition except by a short white space. Aldus did not even insert numbers
to identify chapters in order to present antique texts in their

original format.[12] Only when scholarly editors at the end of the sixteenth century began to print the numbering of the so-called *capita* did things begin to change. French authors then divided their texts into short numbered chapters and subdivided them into paragraphs in the modern sense.

It is interesting here to note the role played in this domain by two important authors, Guez de Balzac and René Descartes. My attention was drawn to this subject by a passage from a letter of Balzac written in 1644: "At your leisure, I beseech you to have copied for me the *Harangue* of La Casa because I wish to include it in my preface at the end of the *Lettres Choisies*. But I would like the letter to be *ex vera recensione Capellani,* and see that the scribe take the pain to divide it into several sections, or (to sound like Rocollet), into paragraphs, as are all my *discours,* which is a great help to anyone who reads them, as it straightens out possible confusion over meaning."[13]

The author of these lines had formerly been involved in the various intrigues of his time but was now living in retirement on his land in the Angoumois. He hoped to have once again the good fortune that would permit him to become Conseiller du Roi, or to phrase it bluntly, to obtain employment as a conseiller from the monarchy. Under these circumstances, the principal goal of his writings was to remind the court's personnel of his existence, and this explains the importance he attributed to the presentation of his books.

Let us examine how he proceeded beginning with the *Oeuvres choisies* of 1628. The author's letters are presented in a single block. This was a constant for published letters in the seventeenth century, and it occurs again in Balzac's *Oeuvres complètes* of 1665. Look next at the edition published in 1631 by Pierre Rocollet, who was associated with Toussaint Du Bray and Claude Sonnius. The *avertissement* is presented in a single piece, but the text itself is divided into paragraphs, which for convenience I shall call *capitula,* that were numbered by Roman numerals in the fashion of modern editions of the ancient Latin classics. Turning next to the edition published by Rocollet in 1634, we see that its title stated explicitly that the text was divided into chapters accompanied by summaries. The concern with aiding the reader is evident. At the same time, the *capitula* are no longer numbered; they had become paragraphs. From this it is clearly evident that Balzac has done everything he can to make his *Prince* attractive. However, it must be noted that each page still contained only around 800 signs, which seems to exclude the possibility of truly rapid reading by the cultivated public of his time.[14]

We come now to Descartes and his *Discours de la méthode.* We know a great deal of detail concerning the publishing history of this work; thus, I shall repeat here only the essentials. This celebrated philosopher was preparing a general work entitled *Le Monde* when the condemnation of Galileo occurred. He then decided to compose a series of essays preceded by a preface that became the *Discours de la méthode.*

It has frequently been observed that it was relatively exceptional to write a philosophical treatise in the vernacular. Perhaps the Inquisition's severity in regard to Galileo may be explained in part by the fact that his *Dialogues* were written in Italian. By choosing to write the *Discours* and subsequently the *Essais* in French, Descartes certainly ran the same risks, which he tried to mitigate by entitling his book *Discours* rather than *Traité* and by omitting his name from the title page. Surely he must have thought that by using French he could circumvent the resistance of learned academics, all partisans of Aristotle and what he called the *Ecole,* by appealing directly to the public of reasonable men, particularly members of the Republic of Letters who occupied important positions in princely entourages. These included his friend Huyghens who was secretary to the prince of Orange. It is understandable that in view of this circumstance his contract reserved two hundred copies for the author that were destined for careful distribution.

For this reason it is also understandable that Descartes did not choose a Parisian printer or an important Dutch printer such as

Elzevir or Blaeu for the publication of the *Discours de la méthode*. Rather, he chose a little-known printer from Leiden, Jean Maire, on whom he could impose his own conceptions. Let us look, therefore, at the edition Maire produced of this famous work. The text of the *Discours* is preceded by a summary describing its organization; on the page opposite the beginning of the text, we read the heading *Première partie* (fig. 10); and the text is broken up into paragraphs (fig 11). In general, one has the impression that Descartes was inspired by the textual format of Balzac's *Prince* and that in any event, like Balzac, he made a great effort to render his work more accessible to a nonspecialized public. This is confirmed by the fact that he did not take the same pains when he published his *Méditationes* of which the Latin text was printed for the most part without paragraphs. This was true both in the Parisian editions, for which he was perhaps not totally responsible, and in the Elzevirian editions, which he could have easily controlled because he resided in Holland.[15]

Thus in the seventeenth century an expanded public with more modern attitudes and often with better mathematical education began to perceive the page in a more synthetic fashion. This occurred in a milieu where the mechanical revolution was unfolding. The young Pascal covered the walls of Paris with his *Essai pour les coniques* (fig. 12); the officers of the royal army were learning to decipher maps and drafts. Latin erudition was in retreat, and, as we have seen, many works were published with titles containing the terms "abbreviated," "essay," or *moyen court*. However, be not deceived: the revolution outlined thus far occurred only slowly. To be sure, the *belles infidèles,* the translations that educated Jansenists readily made of certain patristic or classical texts, were divided into paragraphs in contrast to those made by Amyot in the preceding century. However, the innumerable volumes of *precieux* novels still extended over the length of densely set undivided printed pages. Male and female readers still had to use all their powers of concentration if they wished to follow the thread of a story that they probably read in a murmuring voice. Thus, one can understand better why among a worldly public that loved to converse and where women, judges, and lawyers were accepted as authorities, the most highly appreciated genres were oral. These included the theater, speeches (especially funeral orations), and poetry. All these, and probably letters as well, were designed to be read aloud in the salons. Undoubtedly, the little revolution in paragraph use that I have just described was over by around 1680. It was linked to new ways of reading and of thinking about texts.

DURING THIS SAME PERIOD, Europe, and especially its courts, was becoming conscious of the diversity of its languages. While Latin appeared increasingly to be the language solely of the learned, vernacular literature developed and won for itself authentic credentials. From this came the dream of a common language that would be superior to the spoken word and what it could offer, even when written down. This new common language, one of images, in some sense revived the myth of the original language of which sixteenth-century men had thought they had found traces in the *Hieroglyphics* of Horapollo. This Hellenistic text, brought back in 1519 from the island of Andros near Florence by Cristoforo Buondelmonti, was printed for the first time in 1505 by Aldus Manutius, and it subsequently became the object of numerous illustrated editions.

Such was the origin of emblems, which represented a unique stage in the history of the rapport between text and image. Emblems gave birth to an immense literature whose themes and illustrations were taken up from country to country and that endured at least until the middle of the seventeenth century.[16] The inventor of the emblem book was the jurist Alciati whose *Emblematum liber* appeared for the first time at Augsburg in 1531. It reached its definitive form at Paris in 1534 when the publisher Wechel created the emblem as an intellectual unit by establishing an association between a text and an image within the visual unity of the page. Each of his pages contained three elements: a

title (*lemma* or *inscriptio*), the engraved image (*icon*), and the epigram (*subscriptio*).

We may try to understand how one "read" such a page by examining as an example an emblem from the *Emblematum libellus* of the Flemish doctor Adrianus Junius, published in 1565 by Christopher Plantin at Antwerp. The title *Gloria immortalis labore parta* signifies that immortal glory is the fruit of hard work and anguish (fig. 13). The image that expresses this idea makes use of four coded symbols: the continuous coiled snake is viewed as a sign of eternity, the crown of laurel symbolizes glory, and the shovel and the terrestrial globe symbolize, respectively, labor and human endeavor. If we look above the terrestrial globe (which represents our daily reality), we notice the shovel excavating it. The snake, holding the shovel's handle in his mouth, is encircled by the crown of laurels. Thus, a rhetoric of image identical to the rhetoric of discourse animates the different elements of the emblem, which were placed arbitrarily against a rustic background.

Exciting the mind by their obscurity and polysemantic nature, such illustrations seem to belong to the images employed since antiquity to facilitate memorization and to encourage the creative impulse. The didactic possibilities offered by the emblem were rapidly exploited by spiritual authors. Among them were the Protestant Georgette de Montenay, whose collection of texts was published for the first time in Lyon in 1571, and Arias Montano, the chaplain of Philip II, whose *Humanae salutis monumenta* was published in Antwerp in the same year by his friend Christopher Plantin. This latter work retraces the history of salvation successively through the books of the Bible. The images of Georgette de Montenay's book served to support a discourse of Protestant inspiration that was often theological and polemical. The didactic nature of the text tended to remove all obscurity from the book's emblems as can be seen when the author invites the faithful to drench themselves in the blood of Jesus Christ. In contrast, Arias Montano's work was conceived of as a spiritual book in which an illustrated page is viewed simultaneously with a page containing a *narratio* cast in the genre of a poem of meditation. It is understandable that the Jesuits used this fusion of the art of the emblem with the art of meditation for their own purposes, exemplified by Father Hugo's *Pia desideria* (fig. 14). Strictly following the path of Ignatius de Loyola, Father Hugo tried to furnish the faithful with contexts appropriate to encouraging meditation and the progress of the soul toward God. At the end, he offered the faithful a form of guided oration, as this page exemplifies, in which the emblem is composed of a figure accompanied by a citation from Scripture. It is followed by a poetic meditation, which in turn is followed by a prose commentary composed of patristic citations, the references for which can be found in the margins. These references allowed the reader to place the meditation within the lines of the tradition and the ministry of the Church.

Emblematic literature, which developed principally in Spanish Flanders, succeeded in setting forth the same themes in different European countries. It lent itself to all types of propaganda, utilized, for example, to glorify the Company of Jesus in the famous *Imago primi saeculi* published at Antwerp in 1640, a book recently studied by Marc Fumaroli. This volume, conceived as a festival book, was intended to be a masterpiece of Jesuit spirituality. It proposes to demonstrate that the Company of Jesus developed in the image of the life of Christ. It was constructed "like an architectonic monument with its facade [fig. 15], its peristyle (the dedication), and its six chapels that the reader-pilgrim was to visit one after another and were to be imagined as divided into two groups of three surrounding a central nave. Thus, the reading space battled the abstraction of the printed book to reconstitute, through the arrangement of pages and their illustrations, the experience of the spoken word resounding within an architectural setting."[17]

During these years, however, the emblem began to give way to other techniques of illustration. From the end of the sixteenth century, Cesare Ripa, a member of the Academy of the *Intronati* of Siena, undertook to codify emblematic figures and to confer on them a sort of autonomous existence in his *Iconologia*. Published for the first time in 1593 and translated into French in 1636 (fig. 16), this book had an immense success insofar as it furnished artists with a conventional iconographic repertoire. However, it neglected the polysemantic nature of the emblem and in a way marked its end. Indeed, at about the same time, the substitution of copper engraving for woodcuts obliged publishers of illustrated books to employ a different kind of press for the printing of text than for the engraved illustrations. The result was a progressive rupture between the two. Henceforth, many books were simply illustrated with an allegorical frontispiece that often tended both to summarize the book's objectives and to publicize it.

For our first example, consider Léonard Gaultier's frontispiece for the great edition of the *Oeuvres* of Ronsard (1609, fig. 17). At the apex of a portico within which the title is inscribed, the bust of the poet is crowned by Virgil and Horace. On each side of them, Venus and Mars are meditating. Soon Rubens established himself as the most important master of this genre. Shown here are two of his realizations made for the Plantin-Moretus Press. For the *Poems* of Cardinal Barberini (fig. 18), later Pope Urban VIII, he created a design in which, above a vault whose bay was reserved for the title, he depicted Samson prying apart the jaws of a lion so as to reveal a beehive, an allusion to the arms of Pope Urban VIII and to the sweetness of his poems (1634). The frontispiece illustration became even more complicated in the case of the *Opera* of the spiritual writer Louis de Blois (1632, fig. 19). The title of this work was inscribed on the pages of an open book held by four women representing the four monastic virtues. Kneeling, the author of the book presents his work to Christ and to his mother, enthroned among the clouds accompanied by seven small angels carrying symbolic attributes. Below on the ground are strewn the coats of arms of

Blois, Enghien, Lannoy, et al. The image constitutes a series of symbols and allegories so complicated that they had to be explained in the work's dedication.[18]

Such compositions were singularly complex, and the necessity of incorporating the title on each page obviously further complicated the task of the artist. This explains Nicolas Poussin's reaction to Richelieu's request for a series of frontispieces from the Imprimerie Royale. Practically removing the title from the frontispiece, Poussin placed at the front of Virgil's *Opera* a very simple design representing the poet crowned by Apollo (fig. 20). At the front of Horace's *Opera,* he depicted a muse snatching a satyr's mask from the poet. At the beginning of a large edition of the Bible, he showed God the Father soaring in the sky above two women, one veiled representing the Old Testament, the other woman unveiled representing the New Testament (fig. 21). Thus, in Poussin's illustrations, we have a small number of personages to whom Mellan's burin gave a sculptural look and a quest for simplicity that we may easily interpret as a classical reaction to Ruben's baroque style.[19]

These diverse examples demonstrate that, henceforth, the time had come for book illustration to become the task of artists. Moreover, this trend was not recent. Since the end of the sixteenth century, Antoine Caron, the great painter of celebrations at Fontainebleau, had attempted to illustrate Blaise de Vigenère's *Images ou tableaux de platte peinture des deux Philostrate* in which the author devoted himself to describing what were purported to be Roman paintings.[20] Completed by a team of engravers that included Thomas de Leu, Léonard Gaultier, and Jaspar Isac, these compositions gave rise to a magnificent festival book published by Langelier in 1614. The truly superb engraved title page shows a court celebration taking place in the center of a palace crowned by a dome with long halls aligned on either side (fig. 22). These halls contain the paintings described in the book. One notes in these paintings that each consists of mythological scenes depicted in the manner of emblems, as the example of the scene illustrating the Thyrenians demonstrates (fig. 23).

This work serves to remind us of the importance that was attributed to court festivals throughout this whole period in France as elsewhere, with their masquerades and ballets as well as their dramatic spectacles. We must not forget that a great part of the engraved works of Jacques Callot was made up of veritable visual accounts of these celebrations. Witness his engraving representing an entrance during a ballet presented at the court of Lorraine. Callot's famous *Temptation of Saint Anthony* was inspired by spectacles representing hell that he had seen in Florence.

However, in this period a new type of spectacle conquered France that was open to a larger audience. This was classical theater, and, as we know, Cardinal Richelieu was one of the first to have a permanent stage constructed in France. At the same time, engravers were given the responsibility of creating frontispieces for printed plays. Sometimes, they represented scenes that had actually been performed. At other times, they depicted scenes that for reasons of propriety had merely been described on stage, such as the combat of Horace and Curiace in Corneille's celebrated tragedy (fig. 24).[21]

Such were the diverse elements influencing the illustration of the French classical book, a genre that was at its apogee toward the middle of the century. Let us now examine several examples. First, we have a few engravings evoking pastoral scenes and shepherds. The best examples include the celebrated frontispiece of Honoré d'Urfé's *Astrée* found in the Parisian edition of 1633 and an illustration depicting the hero Celadon throwing himself into the Lignon in spite of Astrée's efforts to stop him. In the background on the left, Celadon is fished out by three nymphs, and a chariot decorated with a round canopy stops near the group. An equally important example is the scene drawn from another novel, Gombauld's *Endimion* (1624), which retraces a very complicated love story inspired by ancient mythology. In it Diana takes on the appearance of the Queen Mother Marie de Médicis. In the foreground, the shepherd Hermodan confesses his love to Diophanie, while in the background, on the right, the Sun disguised as Hermodan appears to Diophanie, and on the left the Sun chases her.

Still another frontispiece of the same class accompanied Tristan's *Plaintes d'Acanthe,* published at Antwerp in 1638. Acanthe, really the Duke of Bouillon, declares his passion to Sylvie, actually the Countess of Berghe, niece of the prince of Orange. Finally, to the above I shall add two more illustrations: the death of Hippolyte taken from Tristan's *Poésie galantes et héroiques* (fig. 25) and that of Actaeon in *Les peintures murales* (fig. 26).[22]

Undoubtedly, an art historian would label as baroque these illustrations taken from works of independent authors of the first part of the seventeenth century. They would say the same about the illustrations of a famous novel, *Ariane,* composed by a protégé of Richelieu, Desmarets de Saint-Sorlin. The frontispiece (fig. 27) very clearly evokes—like so many of the images that I have discussed—the influence of, one could even say the obsession for, the theater, but other images inspired by the painter Vignon's drawings evoke the romantic adventure in a romantic atmosphere that was readily portrayed by the use of chiaroscuro (fig. 28).

This flowering of heroism and romanticism unquestionably corresponded very closely to the atmosphere created by the Fronde. Paradoxically, it seemed to blossom after the Fronde's failure in the novels of Mlle/ . de Scudéry and especially in the great epics that came to the fore after a slow gestation in the 1650s. Consider, for example, an illustration created by Chauveau for Scudéry's *Alaric* showing Lucifer calling the devils to battle (1654, fig. 29). Another, done by Vignon and Bosse for the *Pucelle* by Chapelain (1656), depicts Joan of Arc and Termes riding side by side (fig. 30). Who would dare to predict when looking at these alluring and romantic images that the time for the triumph of classical literature had arrived?

What occurred next? With Scarron and d'Assoucy, the mode of the burlesque became the rage. Consider two scenes borrowed from Scarron's *Le Virgile travesty* (1648–51) based on a scene of the *Aeneid* portrayed in a realist vein. The frontispiece is in the tradition of the Poussin frontispieces that I have previously described (fig. 31). One illustration shows Aeneas carrying his father in a basket. A third view depicts a torture scene. I shall certainly avoid disputing the interpretation of literary historians such as Antoine Adam who explain that the burlesque was considered by the best minds as an agreeable and elegant art form.[23] However, it is likely that the popularity of this mode was evidence of a weariness with the excesses of other genres. How else can one explain the disappearance at this time of the epic and the heroic novel and that the great classical generation of Molière, Racine, Boileau, and La Fontaine cared little about the illustration of their works? Illustration by engraving (this term being taken in a broad sense, as I shall explain) would henceforth be reserved for celebrating the king's glory.

ONE OF MY STUDENTS, Jean-Marc Chatelain, has reminded us that the years 1540–1610 prepared the way for a culture of glory of which the combined political and moral significance began to emerge in the reign of Henri IV.[24] Particularly during the years 1594–1604, the conviction took hold that all things glorious could only occur in the shadow of the king. This belief explains why Richelieu and Mazarin never in any way overshadowed their sovereigns.

Of course, all the resources of the allegory were employed in France, as in England at the time of Elizabeth I, to reinforce the sentiments that engravings were supposed to propagate. For example, examine a pair of engravings taken from the *Sibylla gallica* of Thomas Billon (1624), a collection of anagrams and poetry glorifying Louis XIII (fig. 32). Here Louis XIII and Anne of Austria are represented as Mars and Diana. Another print celebrates Louis XIII's victories after the siege of La Rochelle.

The victory scenes are inscribed in medallions surrounding the statue of the king on horseback, while his enemies are chained to the statue's base. Another example is a royal commission, *Les Triomphes de Louis le Juste,* published in 1649 under the direction of the Liègeois engraver Valdor who was lodged in the galleries of the Louvre.[25] Nothing was spared for a publication in which Corneille collaborated as well as numerous artists such as Della Bella, Daret, and Ladame. It narrates the wars of Louis XIII and includes portraits accompanied by captions to honor the commanders of the royal armies.

Among the plates of this veritable posthumous triumph, first comes the portrait of Cardinal Richelieu and a caption celebrating his exploits. To commemorate the recapture of Corbie, a plate depicts Louis XIII receiving the homage of the vanquished in the company of a helmeted Minerva dressed in a robe bristling with fleurs de lys. The scene occurs in the interior of a tent interlaid with arms. Another plate that accompanies the recitation of the battles fought in Languedoc presents an allegory of blind warfare. A nude man surges out of Vulcan's forge armed with a sword, an oval shield, and a smoking torch (fig. 33); an enormous dragon springs out of a crevice; and in an infernal cave, Discord clamors for weapons. In all, we have a series of themes borrowed from Rubens and the Flemish school of painters. Finally, the volume includes a map of Germany and of a conquered city, which reminds us that war had now become a technical affair that could only be successfully conducted by officers possessing at least a modicum of scientific knowledge.

The most interesting illustration for our purposes, however, is one depicting Hercules, a symbol of France's power, with a shield at his side, decorated with an owl (the bird of Minerva, a symbol of wisdom) as well as other symbolic accessories for the protection of the young king (fig. 34). Henceforth during this troubled period, all attention would be concentrated on the infant-king, who incarnated the future unity and strength of France. All were agreed on the necessity of demonstrating his legitimacy. There is, for example, the engraving in which the Infant Jesus, held in the arms of his mother, entrusts the scepter and crown to the young Louis, who is held by Anne of Austria. In another image, taken from the *Flambeau du juste* of the Capuchin Sébastien de Senlis, the young sovereign, held by his mother, receives the torch mentioned in the title of the work.

Thus, the infant-king Louis XIV grew up in a climate in which the allegorical system, which was beginning to become outmoded, was focused on the celebration of the king's glory. It should not surprise us if, in the end, the king appeared as the last of Renaissance princes. His entrance into Paris following his marriage to the archduchess Marie-Thérèse was the occasion for a particularly solemn reception as an illustration based on an arch of triumph erected at the Saint-Gervais fountain intersection records. The engraving depicts a Temple of the Muses in the form of a mountain pierced by a passageway (fig. 35). In the center of the arch, a medallion shows the profiles of the sovereigns with the caption *Jungit Amor,* while above, Apollo and a chorus of young girls sing in honor of the newlyweds. Subsequently, during the personal reign of Louis XIV, the sovereign's sun emblem and even the design of the château of Versailles, where everything combined to make the king's person and palace the center of the world, constituted the culmination of the theories that were emitting their final and most dazzling light.

Characteristically Louis XIV and Colbert invested colossal sums in the *Cabinet du Roi,* a gigantic engraving enterprise that mobilized the best artists for the task of illustrating the Glorious Monarch's prized treasures and festivities. The result was not mere books, but sumptuous albums of illustrations from which two plates in particular stand out. In one, the king is dressed as a Roman at the time of the *Courses de têtes et de bagues* of 1662. He is placed at the center of a quadrille constituted by the princes of the blood (fig. 36). Another records for eternity the mottos that were adopted on this occasion by a nobility that was now permanently domesticated.[26]

Henceforth, the aim of all celebrations and ceremonies would be to exalt not only the king but also his relatives and his counselors. For example, an engraving of Chancellor Séguier's funeral rites shows an effigy of the deceased enthroned between heaven and earth in a flood of light above his coffin within a church covered with arms and emblems commemorating the chancellor's virtues. However, shortly thereafter in 1683, for the funeral honors of Queen Marie-Thérèse, Jean Bérain destroyed the prevailing baroque conceptions and succeeded in creating a more simple tribute by exploiting the fact that the queen had been an enemy of ostentatious displays and that modesty had always been her principal virtue. Consequently, his scene was dominated by black tones and much light while avoiding too many images.[27]

In fact, from this time on, allegory never again had the same significance and was used simply as a decorative theme during celebrations by a society that had become intrigued with psychology. To the writers of the great classical generation, the text alone sufficed, except perhaps for Bossuet whose funeral orations were pronounced in the middle of the funeral ceremonies that we have seen. However, Bossuet's struggles were, as Paul Hazard has shown, those of the old guard. Henceforth, illustration became documentary, and the only images found at the beginning of books were portraits by artists of the Nanteuil school. A few of the personages represented in this manner included Turenne, the Grand Condé, and also Pascal.

At the same time, the Great King saw himself attacked not only in pamphlets, evidence of the power of the written word, but also in caricatures coming from Holland. Such was the climate in 1702, when royal propaganda, in a final effort, produced its last large illustrated book. Printed in type font specially cut by the engraver Grandjean, the *Médailles du règne de Louis XIV* had been prepared in manuscript by the Académie des Inscriptions.[28] Two of its members, Racine and Boileau, both historiographers of the king, worked with Charpentier and Tallemant on the preparation of the text. The medallions engraved by Varin were reproduced by the best artists of the royal mint, Coypel, Sébastien Leclerc, and Rigaud, while Bérain was placed in charge of the frames. However, this work intended to glorify a declining king was not a success, for it was out of step with its time (figs. 37, 38). Another type of book had already arrived on the scene, exemplified by the *Dictionnaire critique* that Bayle had just published in Holland.

Has the moment come to conclude? Now that I have begun my retirement, I would simply like to pay homage to a book that has never ceased to guide my work, *La crise de conscience euro-péene (1685–1715)*, published in 1935 by a great historian whom I never had the opportunity to know, Paul Hazard.[29] I have basically tried to trace the prehistory of that crisis that is now usually thought to go back to at least 1650. Hazard's book begins with a chapter entitled "An Age without Poetry." Guided by that assertion, I thought I would find the origin of this change in sensibilities, of this triumph of reason and eventually of critical thought, in a progressive reversal of the relation between the spoken word and image, on the one hand, and written letters on the other. This reversal corresponded to a general change in economic conditions that occurred when the north of Europe began to outstrip the south. I also believed that I could detect in this period of crisis in the European conscience a time when written discourse had become autonomous from the spoken word and could thereby lend itself to more objective and lucid analyses of the world, society, and the actions of men, and thus to the development of the critical mind. However, this may be a point of view that is too exclusively French. Other European countries then, as always, were marching to a different tune, a fact that certainly demonstrates the need to proceed to a comparative history of the book. Much work, therefore, remains to be done by my successors.

Conclusion

From the partial history I have just narrated, it is evident that the history of the book much in fashion today is still a newcomer among the fields of recognized research. Early on, the Germans, so proud of having engendered Gutenberg, exhibited an interest in this discipline, and they did so despite political and religious cleavages because of their active bookselling and publishing trades. Yet, historians of the book constituted a world apart whose achievements were often neglected. To be sure, the English and American Shakespearean specialists developed the cult of analytical bibliography, but paradoxically their approach was largely ignored by Continental scholars and was confined to the narrow milieu of librarians and historians of English Renaissance literature. Finally, throughout Europe, bookdealers, publishers, bibliophiles, and librarians have nurtured the cult of fine printing. Yet the "scholarly elite," that is, those who occupy university chairs, have arrogantly scorned the printed archives of our predecessors that comprise Europe's libraries. On the one hand, literary scholars have based their conclusions primarily on an examination of the texts of well-known and carefully selected authors, and, except in Anglo-Saxon countries, they have tended unanimously to view these texts as disembodied and abstract entities whose production and dissemination were the product of a kind of spontaneous generation. On the other hand, European historians who have devoted themselves to the study of archival documents and manuscripts have frequented libraries principally to consult manuscripts, be they memoirs, collections of juridical or political documents, or years of accumulated correspondence.

Everyone acknowledges the debt owed to Lucien Febvre for breaking down so many conceptual barriers. Historians of the book need only follow his example and implement the new techniques of the historical sciences so as to expand our knowledge of documents and research methods. Let us now summarize the principal stages of this as yet unfinished enterprise. In the first stages, confronting a mass of unexploited documents that were often stored in difficult-to-access repositories, scholars utilized techniques of global statistical analysis borrowed from the disciplines of social and economic history. At the same time, they sought to demonstrate that the book was—to employ Febvre's well-known expression—a product, and they attempted to learn about the world of the book. In France, this research was greatly enhanced by the facts that both librarians and archivists were trained at the same institution, the Ecole des Chartes, and that following the French Revolution, French archives were the focus of an endeavor of classification and development without precedent in Europe. Archives relating to book censorship, to the corporation of Parisian booksellers and printers, and to notarial archives have fortunately been preserved. However, the scholars of this early period of 1960–70, perhaps because of the richness of the documentation, lost sight of the fact that the book not only contains a message but also that it is an object that above all needs to be examined in its own right.

New areas of interest began to evolve. Reviving in a way the old history of ideas that had been discarded a bit too hastily in the face of public scorn, the new history of mentalities came into vogue, beginning significantly in 1968, a time of profound soul searching in French universities. Attention turned from printers and publishers to the reader, and the number of works about popular printed literature increased, reflecting diverse ideological preoccupations. Soon interest arose in a problem that had earlier been brought to light by Febvre: how texts functioned as the mental tools of both epochs and individuals. Notice also was directed to the way people read and to the degree to which text format conditioned or reflected modes of reading and techniques for the composition and construction of texts both large and small. At the same time and for the same reasons, interest increased in the conception and perception of book illustrations.

All these different areas of interest stimulated a rapprochement between the history of the book and analytical bibliography, fields that were destined to unite into what was already being called the sociology of reading. The result was a return to the study of the book as an artifact (an approach that I have attempted to follow in this volume) and a new effort to delineate the functions and the status of the author, this somewhat mythical and complex personage who becomes problematic to define when he is no longer equated with the "writer."

Thus, the history of the book has not ceased to evolve over the past thirty-five years. Let us not be mistaken, however. A veritable history of the book will not be written if historians are influenced solely by the latest trends, and new paths of research will prove fruitful only when they take into account earlier achievements and employ a variety of research methods. For example, it is to be hoped that the computerization of the holdings of the great European and American research libraries will one day result in the renovation and refinement of bibliographical statistics. Without question, the quantitative study of terms used in the titles of works will open the way for new technologies and ideas. It will also perhaps one day be possible to measure the percentage of reprints and new releases in the book production of a particular epoch and on that basis better assess the relative roles of tradition and innovation.

In a completely different area, much remains to be discovered in archival holdings. For example, the archives of the Plantin-Moretus Press are awaiting studies that could be undertaken by economic or business historians. In France, the papers documenting the expropriations during the French Revolution contain a mass of unedited information about libraries and the reading habits of the Age of Enlightenment. Moreover, a recently constituted database indicates that essential research concerning the history of publishing in the eighteenth century is still to be done, and it indicates too the location of pertinent unpublished materials. In Italy, the Venetian archives are only beginning to be systematically studied, while in Spain those of the Fairs of Medina del Campo, for example, contain unbelievable treasures. Much work also remains to be done in the archives of Germany and England as well.

However, it is the books themselves that constitute the essential reservoir for future research. It is worth repeating that a scholar cannot claim to deal with the book as an object of study unless he or she has examined a large number of them. Specialists in historical bibliography still often find it impossible to establish the provenances of the numerous books bearing false imprints. Even the most alert historians still frequently overlook commonly used books of a past epoch because today they have for the most part disappeared. The history of text format is only in its beginning stages, although enough is already known for us to believe that one day we will have a better understanding of the structure and mentalities of earlier historical periods in all their diversity, the historical status of texts, and the work methods and strategies of writers.

Thus, today the history of the book continues to evolve in Europe and the United States as reflected in the recent publications of national histories of the book. These general undertakings should not, however, obscure the fact that the essential research often remains to be done and that efforts of analytic reflection must continue. Moreover, the historian who tries to compare the research of his own country with that of his neighbors cannot help but be struck by the apparent divergences in national patterns of development that are solely the result of differences in methods and approaches to the same problems whether the subject be the history of popular literature and its systems of distribution or the history of libraries. However, it must be remembered that the book trade was for a long time restricted to Europe and that the history of the book is destined to enlarge significantly our understanding of the dissemination of ideas. Therefore, if further progress is to be made, it is imperative today to concentrate on what can be called the comparative history of the book. The study of how books circulated and the social function to which they were destined will enhance both our appreciation of the underlying unity of European culture and, by means of statistical analysis, our understanding of why over time one or another nation achieved a fleeting period of dominance. Finally, by the comparative study of text format, we can hope to understand the evolving divergences in the way people thought, divergences that become apparent as soon as one compares books in different languages from a seventeenth-century milieu that was already profoundly marked by national distinctions and where so many new worlds were beginning to appear.

Notes

CHAPTER 1
The Catholic Reformation and the Book (1585–1650)

1. Lucien Lebvre and Henri-Jean Martin, *The Coming of the Book: The Impact of Printing*, trans. David Gerard (London: Verso, 1990; first French ed., 1958), 129–35. See also Jean-François Gilmont, "La fabrication du livre dans la Genève de Calvin," in *Cinq siècles d'imprimerie genevoise (Actes du colloque international sur l'histoire de l'imprimerie et du livre à Genève, 27–30 avril 1978)*, 2 vols., ed. Jean-Daniel Candaux and Bernard Lescazes (Geneva: Société d'histoire et d'archéologie, 1980–81), vol. 1, 89–96.

2. Cf. Philipp Gaskell, *A New Introduction to Bibliography* (Oxford: Clarendon Press, 1972).

3. Léon Voet, "L'offre, diversifacation de la production, tirages, prix des livres: Le cas de l'"Officina Platiniana' à Anvers (1555–1589)" (Istituto internazionale di historia economica "F. Datini," Prato), in *Produzione e commercio della carta e del libro, secc. XIII–XVIII (Atti della Ventitresima Settimana di Studi, 15–20 aprile 1991)*, ed. Simonetta Cavaciocchi (Florence: Le Monnier, 1992), 565–82. See also Henri-Jean Martin, "Comment mesurer un succès littéraire: Le problème des tirages," in *La Bibliographie matérielle (Table Ronde organisée pour le C.N.R.S. par Jacques Petit)*, ed. Roger Laufer (Paris: Editions du Centre national de la Recherche scientifique, 1983), 25–42. Cf. Henri-Jean Martin, "Les tirages au XVIIIe siècle," in *Histoire de l'édition français. Vol. 2, Le livre triom-*

phant, 1660–1830, ed. Roger Chartier and Henri-Jean Martin (Paris: Fayard-Cercle de la Librairie, 1990), 126–27.

4. Richard Gascon, *Grand commerce et vie urbaine au XVIe siècle: Lyon et ses marchands (1520–1580),* 2 vols. (Paris: Mouton, 1972); Nathalie Z. Davis, "Le monde de l'imprimerie humaniste: Lyon," in *Histoire de l'édition française.* Vol. 1, *Le livre conquérant: Du Moyen Age au milieu du XVIIe siècle,* ed. Roger Chartier and Henri-Jean Martin, 2d ed. (Paris: Fayard-Cercle de la Librairie, 1989), 303–35.

5. Henri-Jean Martin, *Print, Power and People in 17th-Century France,* trans. David Gerard (Metuchen, N.J.: Scarecrow Press, 1993), 246–47, 383–90, 481–82. This book was originally published as *Livre, pouvoir et société à Paris au XVIIe siècle, 1598–1715* (Geneva: Droz, 1969).

6. Henri-Jean Martin, *Histoire et pouvoirs de l'écrit* (Paris: Perrin, 1988), 252–53 (a translation by L. Cochrane has been published by the University of Chicago Press).

7. Martin, *Print, Power and People in 17th-Century France,* 2–10, and *Histoire et pouvoirs de l'écrit,* 253–55.

8. Martin, *Histoire et pouvoirs de l'écrit,* 255–57.

9. Martin, *Print, Power and People in 17th-Century France,* 73–87.

10. Leon Voet, *The Golden Compasses: The History of the House of Plantin-Moretus,* 2 vols. (Amsterdam: Van Gendt, 1969–72).

11. *Histoire de l'édition française.* Vol. 1, *Le livre conquérant,* 487–91. For a discussion of Dutch publishing see Roger Chartier, "Magasin de l'univers ou magasin de la République? Le commerce du livre néerlandais aux XVIIe et XVIIIe siècles," in *Le magasin de l'univers: The Dutch Republic as the Centre of the European Book Trade (Papers Delivered at the International Colloquium Held at Wassemaar, 5–7 July 1990),* ed. C. Berkvens-Stevelinck, H. Bots, P. G. Hoftijzer, and O. S. Lankhorst (Leiden: E. J. Brill, 1992), 289–307.

12. Martin, *Print, Power and People in 17th-Century France,* 88–110.

13. Jean-Marc Chatelain, *Livres d'emblèmes et de devises: Une anthologie (1531–1735)* (Paris: Klincksieck, 1993).

14. René Pintard, *Le libertinage érudit dans la première moitié du XVIIe siècle,* 2 vols. (Paris: Boivin, 1943); "Aspects et contours du libertinage," *XVIIe siècle* (1980), 131–61.

15. Christian Peligry, "La pénétration du livre espagnol dans la première moitié du XVIIe siècle (1598–1661)," in *Ecole nationale des chartes: Positions des thèses soutenues par les élèves de la promotion de 1974* (Paris:

Ecole nationale des chartes, 1974), 191–95; "L'accueil réservé au livre espagnol par les traducteurs parisiens dans la première moitié du XVIIe siècle (1598–1661)," *Mélanges de la casa de Velazquez* 11 (1975), 163–76.

16. Martin, *Print, Power and People in 17th-Century France*, 45–59; see the graphs in *Livre, pouvoirs et société*, 1062–66.

17. For more on these topics see Elizabeth L. Eisenstein, *The Printing Revolution in Early Modern Europe* (Cambridge: Cambridge University Press, 1983).

18. Alain Viala, *Naissance de l'écrivain: Sociologie de la littérature à l'âge classique* (Paris: Editions de Minuit, 1985).

CHAPTER 2
Absolutism and Classicism

1. Françoise Robin, "Le luxe des collections aux XIVe et XVe siècles," in *Histoire des bibliothèques françaises: Les bibliothèques médiévales: Du VIe siècle à 1530*, ed. André Vernet (Paris: Promodis-Cercle de la Librairie, 1989), 193–213.

2. Simone Balaye, *La Bibliothèque Nationale des origines à 1800* (Geneva: Droz, 1988), 19–42; Denise Bloch, "La formation de la Bibliotheque du Roi," in *Histoire des bibliothèques françaises: Les bibliothèques médiévales*, 317–28; Ursula Baurmeister and Marie-Pierre Laffitte, "Des livres et des rois: La Bibliothèque royale de Blois" (exhibition catalog; Paris: Bibliothèque Nationale, 1992).

3. Sylvie Charton–Le Clcch, *Chancellerie et culture au XVIe siècle (les notaires et secrétaires du Roi de 1515 à 1547)* (Toulouse: Presses Universitaires du Mirail, 1993).

4. Balaye, *La Bibliothèque nationale des origines à 1800*, 25–42; "La naissance de la Bibliothèque du Roi, 1490–1664," in *Histoire des bibliothèques françalses: Les bibliothèques sous l'Ancien Régime, 1530–1789*, ed. Claude Jolly (Paris: Promodis-Cercle de la Librairie, 1988), 77–83.

5. Annie Parent-Charon, *Les métiers du livre à Paris au XVIe siècle (1535–1560)* (Geneva: Droz, 1974), 40–47; Elizabeth Armstrong, *Robert Estienne Royal Printer: An Historical Study of the Elder Stephanus*, rev. ed. (Abingdon, England: Sutton Courtenay Press, 1986).

6. Annie Parent-Charon, "Humanisme et typographie: Les grecs du roi et l'étude du monde antique," in *L'art du livre à l'Imprimerie Nationale* (Paris: Imprimerie Nationale, 1973), 55–67.

7. Robert Estienne, *Traicté de la grammaire françoise* (Geneva: R. Estienne, 1557); cf. Charles Beaulieux, *Histoire de l'orthographe françoise.* Tome premier, *Formation de l'orthographe des origines au milieu du XVIe siècle* (Paris: Champion, 1927), 247. In the same preface, Robert Estienne says he was inspired to write his grammar by those of Jacobus Sylvius (Jacques Dubois) and Louis Meigret. For a discussion of the grammar of Sylvius published by Robert Estienne with new roman types comprising accents and diacritics, see text at n. 5 in chap. 4.

8. For the exact meaning of this article, see the very important article by Jean-Paul Laurent, *Académie des sciences morales et politiques, Ordonnances des rois de France: Règne de François Ier.* Tome neuvième, *Troisième partie, Mai-août 1539* (Paris: Editions du Centre National de la Recherche Scientifique, 1983), 582–96.

9. Elizabeth Armstrong, *Before Copyright: The French Book-Privilege System, 1498–1526* (Cambridge: Cambridge University Press, 1990).

10. Francis Higman, "Le levain de l'évangile," in *Histoire de l'édition française.* Vol. 1, *Le livre conquérant,* 373–403.

11. Martin, *Histoire et pouvoirs de l'écrit,* 255–56.

12. Bernard Barbiche, "Le régime de l'édition," in *Histoire de l'édition française.* Vol. 1, *Le livre conquérant,* 457–71. For more on the "enregistrement" by the parlements, see also Jean-Dominique Mellot, "Dynamisme provincial et centralisme parisien: l'édition rouennaise et ses marchés (vers 1600–vers 1730)" (Thesis, Université de Paris-Panthéon-Sorbonne, 1992), 99–103 (Geneva: Droz, in press).

13. Henri-Jean Martin, *Print, Power and People in 17th-Century France,* 36–37, 76–82; Denis Pallier, "Les impressions de la Contre-Réforme en France et l'apparition des grandes compagnies de libraires parisiens," *Revue française d'histoire du livre* 31 (1981), 215–73.

14. Martin, *Print, Power and People in 17-Century France,* 38–41.

15. Jean-Marc Chatelain, "Grandeur et gloire en France," in *Ecole nationale des chartes: Positions des thèses soutenues par les élèves de la promotion de 1990* (Paris: Ecole des Chartes, 1990), 35–40.

16. François Fossier, "La charge d'historiographe du seizième au dix-neuvième siècle," *Revue historique* 258 (1977), 73–92.

17. Orest Ranum, *Artisans of Glory, Writers and Historical Thought in Seventeenth-Century France* (Chapel Hill: University of North Carolina Press, 1980); "Richelieu et les historiographes," in *Richelieu et la culture:*

Actes du colloque international en Sorbonne sous la direction de Roland Mousnier (Paris: Editions du C.N.R.S., 1985), 125–38.

18. For the revival of publishing in Paris during the Restoration, see Odile and Henri-Jean Martin, "Le monde des éditeurs," in *Histoire de l'édition française.* Vol. 3, *Le temps des éditeurs* (Paris: Promodis, 1982), 176–221. For the part played by the peddlers in the revival of the world of the book, see also Laurence Fontaine, *Histoire du colportage en Europe, XVe–XVIIIe siècle* (Paris: Albin Michel, 1993), 69–94.

19. Denis Pallier, *Recherches sur l'imprimerie à Paris pendant la Ligue (1585–1594)* (Geneva: Droz, 1976).

20. See also Jeffrey K. Sawyer, *Printed Poison: Pamphlet Propaganda, Faction Politics, and the Public Sphere in Early Seventeenth-Century France* (Berkeley: University of California Press, 1990).

21. *Les Caquets de l'accouchée,* ed. E. Fournier (Paris: P. Jannet, 1855); cf. Martin, *Print, Power and People in 17th-Century France,* 377.

22. Marc Fumaroli, "Le cardinal de Richelieu fondateur de l'Académie française," in *Chancellerie des Universités de Paris et Académie Française, Richelieu et le monde de l'esprit (Sorbonne, novembre 1985)* (exhibition catalog; Paris: Imprimerie Nationale, 1985), 217–35.

23. Gilles Feyel, "Richelieu et la *Gazette,*" in ibid., 207–16; "Richelieu et la *Gazette,*" in *Richelieu et la culture,* 103–24; *La "Gazette" en province à travers ses réimpressions, 1631–1752* (Amsterdam: APA-Holland University Press, 1982); H. M. Solomon, *Public Welfare, Science and Propaganda in Seventeenth-Century France* (Princeton: Princeton University Press, 1972).

24. Martin, *Print, Power and People in 17th-Century France,* 296–310; cf. Bernard Barbiche, "Le régime de l'édition," in *Histoire de l'édition française.* Vol. 1, *Le livre conquérant,* 457–71; for more on the publication of the *Discours de la méthode,* see Henri-Jean Martin, "Les formes de publication au milieu du XVIIe siècle," in *Ordre et contestation au temps des classiques (Actes du 21e colloque du Centre Méridional de rencontres sur le XVIIe siècle jumelé avec le 23e collque de la North American Society for Seventeenth Century French Literature, Marseille, 19–23 juin 1991),* ed. Roger Duchêne and Pierre Ronzeaud (Seattle: Papers on Seventeenth-Century French Literature, 1992), 215–20.

25. See also Paul-Marie Grinevald, "Richelieu et l'Imprimerie royale," in *Richelieu et le monde de l'esprit,* 237–48.

26. Fumaroli, "Le cardinal de Richelieu fondateur de l'Académie française."

27. Viala, *Naissance de l'écrivain: Sociologie de la littérature de l'âge classique.*

28. Fumaroli, "Le cardinal de Richelieu fondateur de l'Académie française." For a discussion of the generalization of the Academic system throughout France at the end of the seventeenth century and in the eighteenth century, see Daniel Roche, *Le siècle des lumières en province: Academies et académiciens provinciaux,* 2 vols. (Paris: Mouton, 1978).

29. Fumaroli, "Les intentions du cardinal de Richelieu, fondateur de l'Académie française," in *Richelieu et la culture,* 69–78.

30. Martin, *Print, Power and People in 17th-Century France,* 383–94.

31. Martin, "Un projet de réforme de l'imprimerie parisienne en 1645," in *Humanisme actif: Mélanges d'art et de littérature offerts à Julien Cain* (Paris: Hermann, 1968), 261–64.

32. Hubert Carrier, *Les Mazarinades,* 2 vols. (Geneva: Droz, 1989–91).

33. Henri-Jean Martin, "Guillaume Desprez, libraire de Pascal et de Port Royal," *Fédération des Sociétés Historiques de Paris et de l'Ile-de-France, Mémoires* (1952), 206–28.

34. André Jammes, "Louis XIV, sa bibliothèque et le Cabinet du Roi," *The Library* 20 (March 1965), 1–12; *Orangerie des Tuileries, 7 octobre 1977–9 janvier 1978: Collections de Louis XIV, dessins, albums, manuscrits* (exhibition catalog; Paris: Editions des Musées Nationaux, 1978); Thierry Sarmant, "Le cabinet des médailles de la Bibliothèque nationale de 1661 à 1848," in *Ecole nationale des chartes: Positions des thèses soutenues par les élèves de la promotion de 1993* (Paris: Ecole des Chartes, 1993), 155–64.

35. Balaye, *La Bibliothèque nationale des origines à 1800,* 100–108.

36. Anne Sauvy, "L'illustration d'un règne: le Cabinet du Roi et les projets encyclopédiques de Colbert," in *L'art du livre à l'Imprimerie Nationale* (Paris: Imprimerie Nationale, 1973), 103–27; Marianne Grivel, "Le Cabinet du Roi," *Revue de la Bibliothèque Nationale* 18 (1985), 36–57.

37. Anne Sauvy, *Livres saisis à Paris entre 1678 et 1701, d'après une étude préliminaire de Motoko Ninomiya* (La Haye: M. Nijhoff, 1972).

38. Paul Mellotee, *Histoire économique de l'imprimerie.* Tome 1, *L'imprimerie sous l'Ancien Régime, 1439–1789* (Paris: Hachette, 1905), 460–66; Martin, *Print, Power and People in 17th-Century France,* 468–78.

CHAPTER 3

The Reading Public and Its Books

1. *Histoire des bibliothèques françaises.* Vol. 1, *Les bibliothèques sous l'Ancien Régime, 1530–1789.*

2. Martin, *Print, Power and People in 17th-Century France,* 333–80.

3. Henri-Jean Martin and Micheline Lecocq, with the collaboration of Hubert Carrier and Anne Sauvy, *Livres et lecteurs à Grenoble: Les registres du libraire Nicolas (1645–1668),* 2 vols. (Geneva: Droz, 1977); cf. Henri-Jean Martin, "Livres et lecteurs à Grenoble au milieu du XVIIe siècle," in *Le Livre français sous l'Ancien Régime* (Paris: Promodis-Cercle de la Librairie, 1987), 187–208.

4. Laurence Fontaine, "Les vendeurs de livres: réseaux de libraires et colporteurs dans l'Europe du sud (XVIIe–XIXe siècles)" in *Produzione e commercio della carta e del libro secc. XIII–XVII,* 631–76.

5. Rudolf Harneit, "Fingierte Druckort: Paris. Zum Problem der Raubdrucke im Zeitalter Ludwigs XIV," *Wolfgenbütteler Notizen zur Buchgeschichte* 14, no. 1 (1989), 1–130, and no. 2, 1–312.

6. O. S. Lankhorst, *Reinier Leers (1654–1714): Uitgever en boekverkoper te Roterdam* (Amsterdam: Maarssen, 1983).

7. Mellot, "Dynamisme provincial et centralisme parisien: l'édition rouennaise et ses marchés (vers 1600–vers 1730)."

8. Romeo Arbour, "Raphaël Du Petit Val et l'édition des textes littéraires en France (1587–1613)," *Revue française d'histoire du livre* 5 (1975), 87–141.

9. For the beginning of the "permissions tacites," see Jean-Dominique Mellot, "Le livre interdit à Rouen," in *Histoire de l'édition française.* Vol. 2, *Le livre triomphant,* 368.

CHAPTER 4

The French Classical Book: Text and Image

1. Thucydides, *L'histoire de la guerre qui fut entre les Péloponésiens et Athéniens,* trans. Claude de Seyssel (Paris: Josse Bade, 1527). Louise de Savoie's copy is kept in the Bibliothèque Mazarine, Paris.

2. Ernest Coyecque, "Josse Bade et les traductions de Claude de Seyssel," *Bibliothèque de l'École des chartes* 4 (1894), 109–14. The contract,

entered into in March 1528 by Josse Bade and Jacques Colin, mentions an issue of 1,225 copies at Colin's expense for the translations by Seyssel of Thucydides (see previous note) and of Diodorus Siculus (see next note) and for two others of Eusebius and Trogus Pompeius that were not made at Josse Bade's.

3. Diodorus Siculus, *L'histoire des successeurs d'Alexandre le Grand,* trans. Claude de Seyssel (Paris: Josse Bade, 1530).

4. Diodorus Siculus, *Les troys premiers livres de Diodore de Sicile,* trans. Antoine Macault (Paris: G. Tory, 1535); the portrait of François I is attribued to Geoffroy Tory; cf. Bibliothèque Nationale, "L'art du livre à l'Imprimerie nationale des origines à nos jours" (exhibition catalog) (Paris: Bibliothèque Nationale, 1951), no. 32.

5. Jacques Dubois, *In linguam gallicam isagoge* (Paris: Robert Estienne, 1532). Actually, Sylvius's method, which was too ambitious, could not be wholly applied. Cf. Nina Catach, *L'orthographe française à l'époque de la Renaissance: Auteurs, Imprimeurs, Ateliers d'imprimerie* (Geneva: Droz, 1968), 39–43.

6. For more on this subject, see text at notes 5 and 6 in chap. 2.

7. Jean Belon, *Histoire de la nature des oiseaux* (Paris: Gilles Corrozet or Guillaume Cavellat, 1555). Cf. Laurent Pinon, *Le livre de zoologie, 1455–1700* (Paris: Klincksieck, in press), no. 21.

8. Lucien Gallois, "La grande carte de France d'Oronce Fine," in *Annales de géographie* 44 (1935), 337–48. Cf. Denise Hillard and Emmanuel Poulle, "Oronce Fine et l'horloge planétaire de la Bibliothèque Sainte Geneviève," *Bibliothèque d'humanisme et Renaissance: Travaux et documents* 33 (1971), 342–43.

9. Terence, *L'Andrie,* trans. Charles Estienne (Paris: A. and P. Roffet, 1542) (a play in five acts and twenty-eight scenes which introduces again the notion of scene into France and is preceded by an important *Epistre du traducteur au lecteur*); *La comédie du sacrifice des professeurs de l'Académie de Sienne, nomméz Intronati, célébrée ès jeux d'un Caresme à Senes: Traduite de l'italien en prose française par Charles Estienne* (Lyon: François Juste and Pierre de Tours, 1543) (a comedy in five acts, thirty-three scenes, and a prologue, and accompanied by an epistle, really a treatise about the theater; the Italian text was published for the first time in 1537, probably in Venice); cf. Bernard Weinberg, *Critical Prefaces of the French Renaissance* (Evanston: Northwestern University Press,

1950), 89–108. Except for such farces as *Pathelin*, only learned or school translations of Terence with the Latin text had been printed in France.

10. For the layout of these books, see Martin, "Les Formes de publication au milieu du XVIIe siècle," 209–24.

11. For the mode of composition of Montaigne's *Essais*, see André Tournon, "Je n'ai jamais lu les *Essais* de Montaigne," in *Le livre I des Essais de Montaigne (Actes de la journee d'étude "Montaigne" du 6 novembre 1992)*, 9–29; "L'énergie du 'langage coupé' et la censure éditoriale," in *Montaigne et la rhétorique: Colloque de St. Andrew, 1992* (in press); George Hoffmann, "The Montaigne Monopoly: Revising the *Essais* under the French Privilege System," *PMLA* 108, no. 2 (1993), 308–19.

12. For instance, see Lactantius, *Opera* (Venice: Manutius, 1535).

13. *Lettres de Jean-Louis Guez de Balzac*, ed. Tamizey de la Roque (Paris, 1873), 578.

14. Martin, "Les formes de publication au milieu du XVIIe siècle," 214–15.

15. Ibid., 216–23.

16. For more on the following discussion, see *Bibliothèque Municipale de Lyon, Livres à figures du XVIe siècle français* (exhibition catalog; Lyon: Bibliothèque Municipale, 1964). For the discussion of the emblem books, the examples are borrowed from Chatelain, *Livres d'emblèmes et de devises*. See also Roger Paultre, *Les images du livre: Emblèmes et devises*, preface by Louis Marin (Paris: Hermann, 1991).

17. Marc Fumaroli, "Baroque et classicisme: l'*Imago Primi saecui Societatis Jesu (1640)* et ses adversaires," in *Questionnement du baroque*, ed. Alphonse Vermeylen (Louvain, 1986), 380.

18. Philipp Hofer, *Baroque Book Illustration: A Short Survey from the Collection in the Department of Graphic Arts* (Cambridge, Mass.: Harvard College Library, 1951). For the frontispieces of Rubens, see J. Richard Hudson and Carl van de Velde, *Corpus Rubenianum: Book Illustration Title Pages*, 2 vols. (Brussels: Aracade, 1977), vol. 2, nos. 61 and 68, and figs. 208–11 and 228–29.

19. For the frontispieces of the Imprimerie royale, see Jacques Thuillier, "Richelieu, son action sur l'Imprimerie royale," in *Richelieu et la culture*, 163–75.

20. Cf. Chatelain, *Livres d'emblèmes et de devises*, no. 160.

21. Pierre Corneille, *Horace, tragédie* (Paris: A. Courbé, 1641).

22. Description of the books quoted here can be found in *Bibliothèque Municipale de Lyon, Livres à figures du XVIIe siècle français*, and in Diane Canivet, *L'illustration de la poésie et du roman français au XVIIe siècle* (Paris: Presses Universitaires de France, 1957).

23. Antoine Adam, *Histoire de la littérature française au XVIIe siècle.* Vol. 2, *L'époque de Pascal* (Paris: Domat, 1951), 79.

24. Chatelain, "Grandeur et gloire en France, 1540–1610," 35–40.

25. J. S. Renier, "Le troisième Valdor, calcographe de Louis XIV," *Bulletin de l'Institut archéologique liégeois* 7 (1865), 123–70; Jeanne Duportal, *Etude sur les livres à figures édités en France de 1601 à 1660* (Paris: Champion, 1914), 285–88. Cf. Odile Faliu, *Jean Valdor de Liège, mémoire de maîtrise* (Paris, 1978).

26. For the Cabinet du Roi see above, chap. 2, n. 36.

27. See also Victor-Louis Tapie, *Baroque et classicisme* (Paris: Plon, 1957).

28. For the "histoire métallique" of Louis XIV, see *Archives de France, L'Académie des Inscriptions et Belles-Lettres, 1663–1963* (exhibition catalog; Paris: Archives de France, 1963), 33–46. The copperplates of the *Médailles des principaux événements du règne de Louis XIV* have been found in the Imprimerie Nationale where they are kept; cf. Bibliothèque Nationale, *L'art du livre à l'Imprimerie nationale des origines à nos jours*, nos. 172–73. For a discussion of the conceiving on that occasion of a new typography under the supervision of the Académie des Sciences, see André Jammes, *La réforme de la typographie royale sous Louis XIV: Le Grandjean* (Paris: Librairie Paul Jammes, 1961; reprint, Paris: Promodis, 1985).

29. Paul Hazard, *La crise de conscience européenne*, 2 vols. (Paris: Boivin, 1935).

Index

Index

Briconnet family, 32
British Library, 6, 21
Burlesque, 92
Budé, Guillaume, 32, 77, 78

Callot, Jacques, 90
Calvinism. *See* Protestantism
Carmelites, 17
Caron, Antoine, 89
Carrier, Hubert, 48–49
Cartography, 25, 28, 79, 84, 93
Catholic Church, policy of
  repression, 12–13
Catholic Reformation, 12–15, 17–
  19, 25, 28, 41–43, 86–87; and
  libraries, 15, 56, 59; pamphlets
  of, 38–39, renewal of Catholic
  piety, 17–19; Spanish influence,
  15, 16, 17; texts of, 42–43
Chapelain, Jean, 61, 91
Charles I of England, 29, 62
Charles V, 31
Charles VI, 32
Charles IX, 37, 57
Chastelin, Jean-Marie, 92
Chatelin, Jean-Marie, 37
Chauveau, François, 91
Classicism, 29, 90; development
  of, 31; theater, 90
Code Michaud (1629), 40
Colbert, Jean-Baptiste, 50–52,
  72, 94
Colin, Jacques, 78
Collège de France, 33
Companie des Usages, 36, 41
Compagnie du Navire, 36, 41
Companie du Très Saint Sacrement,
  64
Conrart, Valentin, 41, 45

Corneille, Pierre, 17, 20, 44, 62,
  65, 90, 93
Corporation of Parisian Printers,
  Booksellers, and Binders, 36,
  46, 98
Counter Reformation. *See*
  Catholic Reformation
Courbé, Augustin, 7
Coypel, Antoine, 96
Cramoisy, Sébastien, 16, 41, 42,
  47, 51–52

Dauphiné. *See* Grenoble
Descartes, René, 25, 28, 41, 82,
  83–84
Desmarets de Saint-Sorlin, Jean,
  91
Dubois, Jacques, 79
Du Petit Val, Raphael, 70
Dupuy Brothers, 43

Ecole des Chartes, 98
Ecrivains, 43–45, 48, 50, 67
Edict of Nantes, revocation of,
  53, 66, 67, 71
Elizabeth I of England, 92
Elzevirs, 16, 67, 84
Emblems, 85–88
Erasmus, Desiderius 13, 64
Estienne, Charles, 79–80
Estienne, Robert, 33, 46, 78, 79
Evangelistes, 32

Fabri, Nicolas, 28
Faculty of Theology (University
  of Paris), 40
Febvre, Lucien, 98–99
Feyel, Gilles, 40
Fine, Oronce, 79

Index

Index

Index

Sales, François de, 43
Scarron, Paul, 20, 44, 62, 92, 93
Scientific publications, 25, 28
Scudéry, Georges de, 61, 91
Scudéry, Madeleine de, 20, 61
Sécrétaire à la mode, 71
Séguier, Pierre, 41, 47, 49, 50, 51, 52, 57, 95
Seneca, Lucius Annaeus, 58
Seyssel, Claude de, 78
Shakespeare, William, 19–20
Spain, 15, 16, 17, 20
Stoics, 58
Straet, van der, Jan, 1
Sublet de Noyers, François, 42

Text format, 79–85, 87; history of, 99, 100, 101
Theresa of Avila, 17
Thomas à Kempis, 61
Thucydides, 78
Tournes, Jean de, 80

Travel literature, 25
Trent, Council of, 13, 35
Type fonts: italic, 80; roman, 77

Universal language, 85
University of Paris, 40
Urban VIII, 41, 43, 88

Valdor, Jean, 93
Varin, Jean, 96
Vatican Library, 56
Venice, early printing in, 6
Vernacular, growth of, 33–34, 77–79, 85
Viala, Alain, 43
Viau, Théophile de, 19, 44
Vignon, Claude, 91
Vitré, Antoine, 19

Wars of Religion, 21, 36, 38
Wechel, Chrétien, 85
Wolfenbüttel Library, 56, 67

Library of Congress Cataloging-in-Publication Data

Martin, Henri Jean, 1924–
    The French book : religion, absolutism, and readership, 1585–
1715 / Henri-Jean Martin ; translated by Paul Saenger and Nadine Saenger.
    p.   cm. — (Johns Hopkins symposia in comparative history ; 22nd)
    Includes bibliographical references and index.
    ISBN 0-8018-5179-3 (alk. paper)
    1. Book industries and trade—France—History—16th century.   2. Book
    industries and trade—France—History—17th century.   3. Book
industries and trade—France—History—18th century.   4. Censorship—
France—History—17th century.   5. French literature—17th century—
    Political aspects.   6. Books and reading—France—History—17th
    century.   7. Illustration of books—France—17th century.   I. Title.
                    II. Series.
            Z305.M27   1996
381'.45002'0944—dc20   95-49135